WHEN POPULISM MEETS NATIONALISM

REFLECTIONS ON PARTIES IN POWER

edited by Alberto Martinelli

ISPI

© 2018 Ledizioni LediPublishing
Via Alamanni, 11 – 20141 Milano – Italy
www.ledizioni.it
info@ledizioni.it

WHEN POPULISM MEETS NATIONALISM. REFLECTIONS ON PARTIES
IN POWER
Edited by Alberto Martinelli
First edition: December 2018

Print ISBN   9788867059003
ePub ISBN   9788867059010
Pdf ISBN   9788867059027
DOI   10.14672/67059003

ISPI. Via Clerici, 5
20121, Milan
www.ispionline.it

Catalogue and reprints information: www.ledizioni.it

Table of Contents

Introduction

Two years ago ISPI published its Report "Populism on the Rise. Democracies under Challenge?". In that book, we looked at how the rise of populist parties and movements had taken the world by storm. In the United States and in Europe, populism was being rediscovered as a loose ideology that could empower opposition parties and movements through a strong, appealing anti-elite message. Yet, despite the election of Donald Trump as the President of the United States, at that moment in time many wondered whether populism would be no more than a passing fad.

In the short span of time between 2016 and today anti-establishment parties in the EU and abroad have made substantial strides. The tactical tool in the hands of opposition parties to bolster their chances against any governing majority by claiming that the latter was the "establishment" and that the oppositions represented "the people", has morphed in a few instances into a full-fledged governmental force. To accomplish this transformation, populist parties had to mix their loose, "thin" ideology with stronger ones: in many cases, the ideology of choice was nationalism.

Today, a number of national-populist parties is in power, in Europe and abroad. Two examples are the League and the Five Star Movement in Italy, or Jair Bolsonaro's rise in Brazil. This is not to say that national-populist parties were not in government before. In Hungary, Viktor Orbán has been in power nonstop since 2010. In 2015, PiS won the election in Poland by adding populist, anti-elite elements to its strand of identitarian politics. And, in 2017, the far-right Austrian Freedom Party joined the government coalition after having moderated its message – thus giving it a much wider appeal – by committing to defend "the common man".

At the same time, one should not infer that national-populist parties today are reaching the levers of government everywhere. In many countries, despite strengthening their electoral support, national-populist parties have been kept effectively at bay by more "traditional" formations. In Germany, the appeal of the far-right Alternative für Deutschland is on the rise, but still limited in a country that retains vivid memories of its Nazi past. In France, the Front National was contained by a two-round electoral system that discriminates against extremist parties. In the Netherlands, the Party of Freedom was excluded from any workable majority, and the same appears to be happening to the Sweden Democrats after this September's election in the country.

Despite all this there is no denying that, today, a larger amount of countries in Europe and abroad is governed by national-populist parties. This rise and consolidation of national-populist parties in the West has given rise to a trend in which the "national-populist" label tends to be applied in a very loose way. Indeed, it is tempting to see all nationalist movements today through the prism of a single, international "national-populist wave". But this would not properly mirror a much more nuanced and complex scenario, with no one-size-fits-all model clearly available.

This Report aims to answer precisely these questions: to what extent can nationalist governments in power in different places in the world be labelled "national-populist"? What are the key ingredients of their success? What kind of policies are to be expected from these governments? Ultimately, what common elements do they share, and in what do they differ?

In the first chapter Alberto Martinelli, the editor of this Report, elaborates on the peculiar features of populist and nationalist ideologies, showing what is likely to happen when the two are mixed together. The March 2018 election in Italy had two clear winners, the Five Star Movement and Matteo Salvini's League. The ideology of the League is a mix of the three classical components of the political right (nationalism, neo-liberalism, and moral/religious conservatism), whereas Di Maio's Five Star Movement seems a manifestation of populist politics, only moderately nationalist. Currently, both parties, are still undergoing an internal transformation. On the one hand, the League is striving to become a fully national party, not so concentrated in the north of the country. On the other, the Five Star Movement is in search of ways to institutionalise its platform and revamp itself, changing from being a movement into a full-fledged political party.

Looking at the United States, Eliza Tanner Hawkins and Kirk A. Hawkins argue that Donald Trump embodies a specific form of national-populism. Namely, through a textual analysis of speeches and debates they find that Trump seems to express an incomplete form of populism that lacks a belief in popular sovereignty. The lack of this element may explain why Trump's popular support has not expanded since the US president came to power (as his most fervent supporters remain based among Republicans), and why it has fostered a radicalisation within the republican party itself. But, at the same time, Trump's strand of national-populism appears to share a common element with other national-populist parties in the world, in that Trump's rhetoric and ruling style did not moderate once he was elected, reflecting the need to be in a permanent electoral campaign mode. Trump's attacks on the media and assertion of executive powers have had a negative impact on American democracy, although not as severe as his worst critics feared.

In other cases, as Radoslaw Markowski puts it in his chapter, national-populist leaders and political parties shift their stances from populism, during the electoral campaign, to a higher degree of nationalism once in power. This is what happened in several Central and Eastern European countries. Markowski analyses national-populist parties in Poland and Hungary, also taking into account political developments in Bulgaria, Slovakia, and the Czech Republic. He argues that intransigent nationalism is on the rise everywhere, and that a shift from populist to nationalist rhetoric is visible in most instances, be it in the Bulgarian Simeon II Movement, the Polish PiS, or the Hungarian Fidesz.

A deep insight into a properly far-right, nationalist party is offered by Karin Liebhart, who retraces the history of the Austrian Freedom Party (FPÖ), which is now in the ruling co-alition with the Austrian People's Party led by Sebastian Kurz. Liebhart claims that the FPÖ underwent many changes depending on whether it was in government or in the opposition. She also argues that the FPÖ finds itself in a better position to influence Kurz's government towards more nationalist stances due to a general shift to the right in Austrian politics.

When moving attention outside the European Union, even more caution is needed when using the national-populist label. As Ilke Toygür explains, Turkey's ruling party, the AKP, could be considered more of a nationalist-conservative than a populist party. Increasingly over the last few years, after the 2016 failed coup attempt, nationalism seems to turn into isolationism, brought into the political discourse by naming and shaming the West and those who did not support the current government, who have come to be considered "enemies of the nation".

An even different mix of nationalist and populist elements is observed in Russia. Eleonora Tafuro Ambrosetti unravels the complex underpinnings of Putin's political project, and explains that both populism and nationalism are used strategically to reach different goals. In particular, Putin adopts more populist stances, such as a direct connection with his electorate, when he strives to boost his popularity, yet he rarely calls for people to act in his support. He also uses nationalist narratives to pursue concrete political goals – for instance, when defending Russian "compatriots" abroad and traditional Russian values, or when coping with international Russophobia.

Sometimes national-populist rulers show autocratic tendencies, which may actually transform and void democratic institutions in some contexts. In their chapter, Carlos de la Torre and Federico Finchelstein look at the blurring lines that separate populism and autocracy in the case of Argentina and Venezuela. The two nations' historical paths demonstrate that populism, even in its left-wing version, might become authoritarian when democratic institutions are weak, and the civil society is underdeveloped.

The bottom line is that the national-populist label today is attributed to parties that have come to govern their countries following different paths and trajectories. To justify the label, a common feature appears to be that national-populist parties need to be in constant electoral campaign mode, and look for ways to mobilise public opinion even when they are governing. But, for instance, in this case Putin's Russia does not appear to fall easily within the nationalist-populist category. And within the European Union, in particular, the stark divide that appeared to be separating Eastern European countries (more prone to strong, nationalist leaders) from Western European countries (more bent on respecting the rule of law) seems to be blurring nowadays.

It is still too early to tell whether national-populist parties will prove resilient to these periods in government. Normally, any party in government tends to lose public support, as it is held accountable for unkept promises. However, the innovative communication strategy of current national-populist parties, centred on harsh rhetorics and repeated attacks on political opponents, might shield these parties during a time in which they need to consolidate their gains. Ultimately, the success of national-populist parties will hinge upon whether the opposition will be able to adapt to a mutated context, but even more on whether and to what extent national-populist parties will be able to deliver on their electoral promises over the coming years.

Paolo Magri
ISPI Executive Vice-President and Director

1. Populism & Nationalism: The (Peculiar) Case of Italy

Alberto Martinelli

Populism is one of the most widely used terms in public debate and media reports, a catch-all word that is applied to different empirical realities. Nationalism is a more established concept of the political lexicon that is often associated with – and sometimes wrongly absorbed by – populism, the most politically relevant of the two. This volume intends to explore the linkage between populism and nationalism in countries where national populist parties are in power. Most chapters focus on Europe, one on the United States, and another one on Latin America, in order to show analogies and differences on the two sides of the Atlantic. The aim of this introduction is to outline the key features of both populism and nationalism and the main causal factors of their rise in contemporary Europe, to discuss the special case of the Italian coalition government between the League and the Five Star Movement (FSM for short), and to reflect on the role of national populist parties in the future of the EU.

Nationalism

Nationalism is a key concept in the political lexicon of modernity[1]. Although polysemic, ambiguous, changing in time and

---

[1] J. Breuilly, *Nationalism and the State*, Manchester, Manchester University Press, 1982.

space, the concept connotes a defined and well-structured ideology with a strong emotional appeal; it has been a powerful factor in shaping mass political behaviour and has characterised the political struggles of the last two centuries. Nationalism can be defined as the ideology, or discourse, of the nation. It fosters specific collective movements and policies promoting the sovereignty, unity, and autonomy of the people gathered in a single territory, united by a distinctive political culture and sharing a set of collective goals. The concept of nationalism is strictly related to that of the nation-state; on the one hand, nationalist ideology coordinates and mobilises collective action in nation-building through the sentiment of belonging to the nation as a primary identity, while, on the other hand, the centralisation of power in a sovereign state (i.e., the unification of territory, language, culture, and tradition) allows nationalist ideology to prevail over the many regional/local cultures and identities of pre-modern societies. Nationalism is the political principle that affirms the necessary congruence between political unity and national unity and helps to achieve the political project of the fusion of state and nation. The conception of the nation-state as a natural state was successful in mobilising the people for defense against foreigners, but also for legitimising aggressive expansionism.

Nationalism is historically specific. It is a basic aspect of the culture and institutions of modernity, although, both as an ideology and a political movement, re-elaborates pre-modern symbolic materials, such as ethnicity, with the aim of forming a new collective identity and solidarity in a modern society of individuals. By performing the three key functions of legitimacy, coordination, and mobilisation, nationalism has played a key role in responding to the crucial question of how modern societies can establish an effective state-society connection and reconcile the public interest of citizens with the private interests of selfish individuals.

Nationalism is a modern phenomenon also because it is closely related to the interconnected set of economic, political, and socio-cultural transformations that characterise the various roads toward and through modernity (industrialisation, bureaucratisation, democratisation, mass communication). The role of nationalism varies in the different roads to modernity[2], but there are common processes and recurrent features[3]. Modern industrial societies require in fact the free movement of labour, capital, and goods throughout the national community, universal schooling and a standardised national language, intensified social and geographical mobility. By stressing the idea of common citizenship (i.e., the nation as the body of citizens who participate in liberal-democratic institutions), nationalism meets the need of securing cohesion in the face of fragmentation and disintegration caused by rapid industrialisation. It is reinforced by the development of mass politics when the insertion of hitherto excluded social groups into politics creates unprecedented problems for the ruling elites, who find it increasingly difficult to maintain the loyalty, obedience, and cooperation of their subjects and try to secure the support of the masses by providing a common cultural identity for members of different social groups. Moreover, nationalism helps to develop a national culture by destroying both the exclusiveness of elite high cultures and the parochialism of local cultures[4]. And it grows through the development of primary education, the invention of public ceremonies, the mass production of public monuments, to the point of becoming a new secular religion.

The XIX century and the first half of the XX century were the age of the irresistible rise of nationalism. The nationalistic fever did not decline among the peoples of Europe after the useless slaughter of the Great War; to the contrary, it reached a new apex with the advent of totalitarian regimes and the global conflagration of the Second World War. Only the death of tens

---

[2] L. Greenfeld, *Nationalism: Five Roads to Modernity*, Cambridge, Harvard University Press, 1992.
[3] A. Martinelli, *Global Modernization. Rethinking the Project of Modernity*, London, Sage, 2005.
[4] E. Gellner, *Nations and Nationalism*, Oxford, Blackwell, 1983

of millions, the shame and horror of concentration camps, and the enormous destruction perpetrated by the war induced peoples that had fought against each other for centuries to put an end to the "European civil wars", establish peaceful relations, and outline the supranational regime of the European Union.

After the end of the Second World War, nationalism did not disappear in the world but took other forms, first of all in the anti-colonial independent movements of Africa and Asia. At the twilight of the 20th century, it strongly re-emerged in Europe as well, where the collapse of the USSR caused the explosion of ethnic, religious, and national conflicts and tensions that had been latent and to a great extent absorbed into the Cold War confrontation between the two superpowers. The surfacing of these old conflicts got linked with the new conflicts stemming from the economic and political changes which took place in the post-Soviet world.

Nationalist parties and movements in Eastern Europe are not, however, the only instance of resurgent contemporary nationalism in the Western world: in the early XXI century, national populism is growing in the US – as testified by Donald Trump's victory – and in many European countries – as showed by the upsurge of national populist, anti-EU, parties – as a reaction to the threat of deterritorialisation and uprooting caused by globalisation and as a response to the problems raised by the economic financial crisis and the poor functioning of representative democracy both at the Union and at member state levels[5].

Populism

Even more polysemic and controversial than nationalism is the concept of populism, which refers to a wide range of empirical phenomena. It has been defined as a rhetorical style of political communication, a thin-centred ideology[6], a form of political

---

[5] A. Martinelli, *Beyond Trump: Populism on the Rise*, Milan, Epoké-ISPI, 2016, p. 15
[6] C. Mudde, *Populist Radical Right Parties in Europe*, Cambridge, Cambridge

behaviour, and a strategy of consensus organisation. Although present in the language of almost all political leaders as a rhetorical style and an attempt to connect empathically with the masses, populism acquires the features of a full-fledged ideology when the political discourse is organised around a few core distinctive features: the two concepts of "people" (as the legitimate source of power) and "community" (as the legitimate criterion for defining the people), the antagonistic relationship between two homogeneous groups, *We* (the pure, virtuous people) and *Them* (the corrupt, inefficient, and negligent elite or establishment); the absolute right of the majority against the minority; the denial of pluralism and intermediation.

The linkage with nationalism can be explained by the fact that the vagueness and plasticity of this ideological core, thin and strong at the same time, allows the populist rhetoric to be combined with a variety of more elaborated, "thicker", ideologies, such as nationalism[7] or leftist radicalism, that add more specific content to it. In other words, conceiving populism as a thin ideology illustrates the dependence of populism on more comprehensive ideologies that provide a more detailed set of answers to key political questions[8]; moreover, it allows to account for the variety of political content and orientation of populist movements (right and left), while simultaneously stressing a set of common features. The right or left orientation depends on: defining who are the "people" (the sovereign "demos") – that is, the legitimate foundation of the political order; the people-mass, the common people – that is, opposed to the oligarchy; the people-nation with its ethnic roots[9]; and on deciding who should be included or excluded from the people and on which elites or minorities put the blame, besides traditional party leaders (foreigners, asylum-seekers, specific immigrant groups for rightwing

University Press, 2007.

[7] P.A. Taguieff, "La doctrine du national-populisme en France", *Etudes*, Janvier 1986, pp. 27-46.

[8] B. Stanley and P. Ucen, *The Thin Ideology of Populism in Central and Eastern Europe: Theory and Preliminary Mapping*, unpublished, 2008.

[9] Y. Meny and Y. Surel, *Par le peuple, pour le peuple*, Paris, Fayard, 2000.

populists; global financial oligarchy, transnational elites, for left-wing populists; Eurocrats for both). But boundaries are blurred, and several ideological elements cross the left/right cleavage, like the mistrust of any elite (first of all the political elite), the emphasis on the people as the true legitimate actor of public decision-making, the rejection of pluralism and institutional intermediation, the stress of communitarian bonds – which goes often together with the diffidence and refusal of others (immigrants, strangers, ethnic minorities, worshippers of other religions); the defense of localism against cosmopolitan culture and sometimes the sheer rejection of modernity; the lack of ethics of responsibility (in Max Weber's sense) as far as the consequences of ideological claims are not taken into consideration; the downplaying of expertise, scientific knowledge, and complexity in favour of simplistic solutions.

The ideology with which populism is more often linked is nationalism; it is also the riskiest for liberal-democracy since it can imply violent conflicts and an authoritarian drift. Although not present in all forms of contemporary European populism, the link with nationalism reinforces and organises the populist ideology around the key questions of inclusion into/exclusion from the community and of the re-affirmation of national sovereignty against the EU "super-state" in opposition to the project of "an ever-closer union". There is a widespread belief that some immigrant groups are culturally incompatible with the native community and are threatening national identities; the EU institutions are blamed for fostering this threat by upholding the free movement of people. Nationalism and populism in today's Europe have a lot in common (the demonisation of political opponents, a conspiratorial mindset, the search for scapegoats, the fascination with more or less charismatic leaders), but, first and foremost, they share the anti-EU stance. The hostility toward the European project of greater political integration, the opposition to the euro, and anti-Europeanism in general, are the connecting link between populism and nationalism, where nationalism and populism merge. The national-populist strategy of collective mobilisation and consensus formation makes an instrumental use of the popular resentment against the establishment and the allure of anti-politics and pits national sovereignty against European governance. EU institutions are often the main scapegoat and critical target; but national elites are criticised too, for being unable to oppose Europe's supranational technocracy or even for being their accomplices, affirming that they must, therefore, be replaced by the true defenders of national interest[10].

The relationship between the national principle and the democratic principle has evolved in a complex and sometimes contradictory way. Populism is against political pluralism and is the permanent shadow of representative politics[11]. In contemporary Europe, national populists are not anti-democratic and actually claim to be the true interpreters of democracy; but they have an illiberal conception of democracy that stresses the democratic component ("government of the people, by the people, and for the people", the absolute power of the majority) at the expense of the liberal component (division of powers, constitutional guarantees, institutional checks and balances, minority rights)[12]. Populists uphold a notion of direct democracy that attributes absolute power to the majority, thus opening the way to what Tocqueville defined the "dictatorship of majority rule".

National-Populism in Contemporary Europe

I have already analysed[13] the main causal factors of the rise of national-populism in contemporary Europe; I will only briefly summarise them here. The causes of the upsurge of national

---

[10] A. Cavalli and A. Martinelli, *La società europea*, Bologna, Il Mulino, 2015.

[11] H.W. Muller, *What is Populism*, Philadelphia, University of Pennsylvania Press, 2016.

[12] N. Urbinati, "Democracy and Populism", *Constellations*, vol. 5, no. 1, March 1998, pp. 110-124.

[13] A. Martinelli, *Mal di nazione. Contro la deriva populista*, Milan, Università Bocconi Editore, 2013; Idem (2016); Idem, "Sub-national Nationalism and the catalan Puzzle", in A. Colombo and P. Magri (eds.), *Big Powers Are Back. What About Europe?*, Milan, Ispi, 2018.

populism in Europe are only partially similar to those at work in other regions of the world, as the second chapter by Eliza Tanner Hawkins and Kirk Hawkins and the last one of this volume by Carlos de la Torre and Federico Finkelstein show. European national-populist leaders – from Hungary Fidesz' Viktor Orban to Poland PiS's Jaroslaw Kaczynski, from Italy Lega's Matteo Salvini to France Front National's Marine Le Pen, from Ukip's Nigel Farage to Alternative fur Deutschland's Frauke Petry, from Dutch Freedom Party's Geert Wilders to Swedish Democrats' Jimmie Akesson – have been encouraged by Donald Trump's victory, They welcomed his victory as the sign of new times and new opportunities for the majority that has been betrayed by globalisation, and they agree with Trump's protectionism and demagoguery ("made in America", "buy American", "power back to the people"). One cannot, however, exaggerate the similarities between European and American politics, since European populism also has specific features that combine in different ways in the various EU member states.

The diffusion of national-populism has been favoured by past long-term processes, like modern nation-building, the advent of mass politics, colonialism, and decolonisation: but some interrelated causes have contributed to its strong comeback on the political stage in contemporary Europe.

The first group of causes that favour the rise of national populism concerns the pathologies of representative democracy and the crisis of its main actors: political parties. Representative democracy works well when a government, legitimised by the free vote of the majority and accountable to all citizens, can effectively manage complex issues. Today, both legitimacy and efficiency are in crisis: on the one hand, mainstream political parties are less and less able to mobilise voters and structure political conflict; on the other, globalisation erodes national sovereignty and limits the capacity of national governments to implement effective policies, while the EU governance system does not have yet the legitimacy and scope of action necessary to deal with problems too big to be coped with at the national level.

This double crisis has been going on for decades. Traditional mass parties have been losing consensus and influence as a result of different, interrelated processes of change: first of all, the declining appeal of great ideological narratives, the failure of communism with the collapse of the Soviet Union, the helplessness of social democracy in the face of growing inequalities, and the boiling down of liberalism to a self-regulating market doctrine. The great cleavages – both political-cultural (state vs. church, centre vs. periphery) and socio-economic (land vs. industry, capital owner vs. worker) – that marked the formation of the modern European society and gave birth to traditional parties were weakened by the combined impact of secularisation, the growth of the service economy, the feminisation of the workforce, and the extension of welfare. Together, these processes lessened class and religious conflicts and undermined the traditional bases of mass parties. Then, economic and cultural globalisation deepened and amplified the transformation.

Contemporary globalisation has put a heavy strain on the institutions of representative democracy, governments, parliaments, parties. Globalisation is characterised by the contradiction between growing economic interdependence at the global level and persistent political fragmentation of the world system into sovereign nation-states. Globalisation creates new technological and economic opportunities, but also growing inequalities; by distributing costs and benefits unequally, it fosters new cleavages in society between those social groups that are (or perceive to be) favoured by the global economy and a multi-ethnic society and those that are (or perceive to be) harmed; and these new cleavages exacerbate a misalignment between traditional parties and their voters. Traditional parties seem less and less capable of channeling, filtering, and processing the increasingly fluid and heterogeneous demands coming from civil society, with the result that the proposal of coherent government programmes becomes more and more difficult. Until the 2008 global financial crisis, the opportunities of globalisation seemed to outweigh the costs, not only for the United States and Asia's big emerging economies but also for the EU; but after 2008, the balance has reversed with economic stagnation, unemployment, and sovereign debt severely affecting EU countries, which recovered only recently.

Globalisation has created problems not only for representative democracy but for performing democracy as well. More than three decades of globalised economy have eroded the sovereignty of the nation-state (which has been the context in which modern democracy has developed); reduced the range of government policy options and their effectiveness (thus further enlarging the gap between what is promised by leaders and what is delivered); implied a shrinking and redefinition of the welfare state; jeopardised the traditional intermediary role of parties, unions, business organisations, and professional associations; and fostered citizens' distrust of leaders and disaffection for democratic institutions. In the European Union, the erosion of the national sovereignty of member states could be compensated by supranational governance, but this happened only to a limited extent because the Union is still unaccomplished and suffers from a democratic deficit.

The second set of causes stems from the impact of the post-Cold War scenario that brought to light old cleavages and old nationalisms and created difficult problems of regime change, thus fostering the political career and access to power of national-populist leaders and parties in those Central and Eastern European countries that in the 45 years after the Second World War had experienced limited sovereignty, authoritarian regimes, and planned economies. The implosion of the Soviet Union has reopened cleavages and conflicts that during the long Cold War had been absorbed into the bipolar confrontation between the USA and the USSR. The end of the struggle between two alternative *Weltanschauungen* helps explain the resurgence of national, ethnic, and religious identities – with the related geopolitical conflicts – that had been anesthetised and hidden behind the rhetoric of universalistic ideologies (free society and communism).

Old cleavages inherited from the past intersect, and partly

overlap, with the new conflicts stemming from the political, economic, and cultural transformations of the present and the new global processes. With the collapse of the ancient regime, when the planned economy and social security system break down, traditional social relations are in flux and sentiments of general insecurity grow, ethnic groups are brought to rely on their cultural and linguistic communities. Where society fails, the nation seems the only guarantee, and national populism prospers. Moreover, the Eurosceptic attitude of many leaders and citizens of countries like Poland, Hungary, the Czech Republic, and Slovakia can also be traced to the reluctance to give up (if only partially) their recently regained national sovereignty to supranational institutions. The four countries forming the Visegrad Group share a notion of the EU "à la carte": they gladly accept the financing of the EU's social cohesion policy but refuse to accept the agreed quotas of asylum-seekers within their national borders.

The third main root cause is the global financial crisis and economic stagnation that amplified globalisation's negative impact on given social groups (low-skill workers in traditional industries with diminishing wages, unemployed and underemployed youth finding only precarious jobs, and other "globalisation losers") and fueled the opposition against migrants who compete for jobs with the natives and against transnational corporations that cut jobs at home through offshoring (a major propaganda item in Trump's electoral campaign). The prolonged economic-financial crisis and the growing unemployment and underemployment fostered a climate of psychological uncertainty, fragmentation, and precariousness that favours resentment and protest.

Mainstream government parties, already under stress, have become the target of national-populist propaganda that portrays them as the docile instruments of supranational technocratic and financial elites. For Marine Le Pen's Front National, for instance, "*mondialisme*" is the new contemporary slavery, and the vagrant, anonymous bosses of international finance are

the "new slave-traders", who in the sacred name of profit want
to destroy everything that tries to oppose their tyranny – first
of all, the identity and sovereignty of the nation. The euro is
involved in the condemnation and defined as treason not only
to France but Europe at large since it implies the forced integration of European economies into a US-dominated world
market. Together with global elites, the EU superstate, and the
euro, immigrants are easy scapegoats: the protracted crisis re-
vives the denunciation of migrants stealing jobs and welfare
subsidies from the indigenous population. National-populist
parties in many European countries – like the Ukip, Italy's
Lega, the Finns Party (formerly known as the True Finns), the
Dutch People Party, the Flemish Vlaams Belang, and Austria's
Freedom Party – uphold policies of welfare state chauvinism
that restrict social protection only to natives[14].

The anxiety related to the long economic crisis intersects
with the implications of Middle Eastern wars and African failed
states (the pressure of asylum-seekers who escape from war, political instability and social disintegration, the terrorist attacks of
Islamic fundamentalism against European cities), fosters a dif-
fuse sense of insecurity and fear for the future, and creates a favourable ground for anti-establishment parties and movements.

Fourth, the rise of national populism can be traced, last but
not least, to the cultural dimension of globalisation – namely
the explosion of digital communication, which has amplified
the role of mass media in the political space. Traditional media,
and commercial television, in particular, have exerted a significant influence in politics, in so far as they contributed to increasing the costs of electoral campaigns and strengthening political
lobbies, personalising leadership, weakening internal party di-
alectic, and depoliticising mass protest. Communication spe-
cialists have replaced party cadres. The marketisation of mass
media dictates its own logic, to which political actors have to

---

[14] H. Kitschelt (with A.J. McGann), *The Radical Right in Western Europe*, Ann
Arbor, Michigan, University of Michigan Press, 2000.

adapt. Televised talk shows treat politics as any other message, fulfilling the need of capturing the viewers' attention by turning everything into something spectacular, oversimplifying and overdramatising every issue, stereotyping and demonising rivals, reiterating scandals and personal accusations. Commercial TV appears in line with the populist rhetoric of glorifying the common sense of the average person, even when it equals prejudice, disinformation, and false messages.

The new digital media turned out to be even more influential than television[15]; they have further weakened political parties' capacity to mediate and intermediate and undermined the authority of scientists and intellectuals. Authority based on knowledge and experience is challenged daily by millions of web users who pretend to be experts on everything and are perennially indignant. The refusal to listen to the opinion of experts or to verify the reliability of a presumed scandal is part and parcel with the populist distrust and hostility toward any type of elite, including the intellectual elite, with the consequence that many people are victims of false news, covered manipulations, conspiracy theories, and post-truths. An alarming picture: the digital revolution offers many opportunities but also raises worries for the quality of public discourse. Blogs and social networks are seldom used in order to better the knowledge of reality, to develop the critical mind, to experiment with forms of deliberative democracy, to educate citizens to respect different opinions and be open to dialogue, debate, and compromise. The Internet is, on the contrary, more often used for naming and shaming, making up scapegoats, expressing frustrations and prejudices, complaining while putting the blame always on others for misdoings and failures in a game of collective rejection of personal responsibility. The field is thus open for the diffusion of messages with a strong and immediate emotional impact, such as those of nationalism, populism, and anti-Europeanism

---

[15] H. Kriesi and T.S. Pappas (eds.), *European Populism in the Shadow of the Great Recession*, Colchester (UK), ECPR Press, 2015.

National Populism in Italy

This volume is about national populism in government. What happens when populist parties get to power? Do they show a clear discontinuity from their electoral/opposition past? Do they set an ephemeral agenda? Do they emphasise core populist topics (polarisation people/elites, scapegoating, conspiratorial beliefs, simplism), or do they strengthen their nationalist component, compensating for their weak populist one? Populist parties in government, becoming the new elite, tend to underplay the core "people versus elite" ideological item or to shift blame on previous governments and traditional elites. But there is more. Populists display strong ethics of conviction but weak ethics of responsibility (in Max Weber's sense), i.e., they underestimate the consequences of their ideological claims and government policies. This attitude can help winning elections insofar as allows to make promises although knowing that they can hardly be fulfilled, but it cannot hold in government policy-making. The complementary attitude of simplism is also under strain when these parties are in power. For leaders who proclaim that the key problems of the country are not complex and difficult to manage but just require simple, univocal solutions, that experts are useless since people wisdom is enough, that for problems to be solved voting the "right" people is enough, it is hard to explain to voters, once elected, that their promises have to be watered down, delayed, or utterly forgotten, that proclaimed party "values" no longer apply and external constraints (like the reaction of financial markets or the criticism by the European Commission) must be taken into account, and technocrats have to be recruited. A common way out from these contradictions is blame shifting; national populist parties, when in power, try to persuade supporters that election promises cannot be fulfilled because of the negative legacy of previous governments, narrow-minded Eurocrats, selfish international investors, and envious foreign countries, often adopting conspiracy theories of various kind. The linkage with nationalism plays an important role in this respect since potential scapegoats are often foreigners and the appeal to close ranks against aliens reinforces the shaking consensus due to unfulfilled promises. In the following pages, I will focus on the special case of the Italian coalition government between the League and the FSM.

In Italy today populism is more evident than nationalism; the latter is strong in the League but rather weak in the FSM. After the advent of the so-called "Second Republic" in 1994, there were three main instances of populist parties: Silvio Berlusconi's Forza Italia, Umberto Bossi's Lega Nord, and Beppe Grillo's Five Stars Movement. Forza Italia has been the forerunner of populism through the widespread use of populist rhetoric in speeches, newspaper articles, and television talk shows, but Berlusconi has now become himself a victim of a more updated, aggressive type of populism. The new Lega (League) led by Matteo Salvini, who has transformed Bossi's separatist Northern League into a nationalist party is attracting many of former Berlusconi's followers. I will focus my attention on Salvini's League and Luigi Di Maio's FSM, after briefly discussing to what extent Berlusconi can be considered a populist leader.

Berlusconi and his "Forza Italia" party presented some of the distinctive characters of populism but lacked others. Berlusconi entered Italian politics presenting himself as a newcomer, eager to get rid of the baroque rituals of existing mainstream parties, which were either disappearing under the blows of judicial investigations – like Christian Democracy (DC), the Socialist Party (PSI), the Republican Party (PRI), and the Social Democratic Party (PSDI), or deeply transforming themselves – like the former Communist Party (Partito Democratico della Sinistra PDS). Berlusconi promised to change Italy for the better, as he had successfully done with his business, and simplify and speed up government decision-making, by adopting a managerial style. However, although opposing the old political elite and competing with the economic-financial elite, he never took a clear anti-elite stance; on the contrary, he co-opted the elites into the new power system. It was not the "people" against the establishment, but his supporters against his political opponents. His media empire contributed to polarise and antagonise public debate, as well as personalise political competition but, at least in the first phase, Berlusconi built his consensus on the Italian citizens' hopes for a more prosperous future rather than on their frustrations and fears. Only afterward, after the poor performance of Forza Italia-led governments in the early XXI century and under the impact of the economic recession, the sovereign debt crisis and immigrant pressure, the propaganda of his party changed and started exacerbating feelings of fear and insecurity, searching for scapegoats and relying on blame shifting. However, this consensus strategy was, in the end, more effectively and ruthlessly pursued by the new League of Salvini. One could say that Berlusconi contributed much to the upsurge of populism in Italy but is no longer its primary beneficiary.

The March 4, 2018 election marked the success of populism in Italian politics, although its rise started earlier and was prepared by structural and cultural transformation in Italian society: first, the crisis of mainstream parties as the key aspect of the more general crisis of representative democracy[16] that can be traced – among other things – to a generational change in the electorate, i.e., the gradual substitution of old voters (with strong ideological attachment, stable party affiliation, and a more structured position in society) with younger voters (who are more volatile, ideologically uncertain, and live a more precarious social condition). Second, the increasing precariousness of working and family life, that affected not only the young but a growing number of people, as a result of the uneven distribution of the costs and benefits of globalisation, with the related feelings of uncertainty and resentment among the "globalisation losers". Third, precariousness and resentment were intensified by the global financial crisis and the fiscal austerity measures required by European institutions and implemented

---

[16] A. Martinelli (2018).

by member states' governments to cope with it. Fourth, a growing feeling of insecurity, related to immigrant pressure, that, on
the one hand, was exaggerated by populist propaganda, but, on
the other, was largely neglected and misunderstood by leftist
parties as a key factor in shaping voters' preferences. Fifth, the
impact of judicial investigations on corrupted politicians and
of citizens' protest against the political class' recurrent scandals,
intolerable privileges, and detachment from ordinary people's
problems (as it is shown by the very low level of public trust for
parties and parliament members in opinion polls). Popular protest was fostered by a pounding "anti-caste" media campaign
that put the blame of inefficiency and corruption on the political class as a whole and was transformed by the League and
the FSM into a radical antagonism between the "people" and
every type of elite. Finally, the impact of the new digital media,
Facebook and Twitter, that proved to be even more powerful
than television in changing the style of political communication and influencing voters attitudes.

Mainstream parties did not adequately interpret these changes. On the centre-right of the political spectrum, Forza Italia
could not fully exploit the anti-EU, neo-nationalist sentiment
because of its ties with the European People's Party. On the centre-left, the Democratic Party neglected the pleas of the poorest
social groups, focused on upholding civil liberties over traditional class interests, and, until recently, did not effectively cope
with the immigrant question. Moreover, mainstream parties
stubbornly resisted to relinquishing their privileges and control
of key resources and became increasingly disconnected from society, although they continued to look very powerful in the eyes
of citizens, as key components of the state apparatus, which use
public media to recruit personnel from the state bureaucracy
and distribute public resources and benefits to their supporters,
thus fostering the populist "anti-caste" propaganda. All these
factors contributed, in different combination and to different
degrees, to the rapid upsurge of the FSM and the League, that
were able to present themselves as new political actors through

skillful use of social media and a renewal of grassroots politics.

The March 4, 2018 election had two clear winners, the FSM (with 32.68% of the vote in the Chamber and 32.2% in the Senate) and the League (with 17.37% in the House and 17.62 in the Senate). Voters showed a high volatility: more than one fourth of them (26.7%) made an electoral choice different from the one they made in the previous 2013 national election (when an even higher percentage of voters, 37%, had changed their preferences), despite the fact that the competing parties were almost the same.

The two winners are both similar – as instances of populist politics – and different – in terms of voters, ideology, and programme priorities[17]. When Salvini took control of the party, he made a complete turnaround from the Lega Nord – a regional party that demanded greater autonomy for Northern Italy within a federal state (and, from time to time, even threatened to secede from Italy), targeted Southern Italians as assisted clients of patronage welfarism, and blamed Rome as the site of political corruption ("Roma ladrona") – to the League, a right-wing nationalist party designed on the model of Marine Le Pen's Front National, with strong ties with the Visegrad Group countries' governments, that builds its consensus on the security issue, the promise to stop immigration, and the opposition to the European Union. The ideology of Salvini's League is a mix of the three classical components of the political right: nationalism, neo-liberalism, and moral/religious conservatism. The League, like other national right-wing parties, is nationalist in the sense of "putting the interests of Italians first" both with regard to immigrants and European institutions. The inflow of immigrants should be stopped or strongly reduced since they are considered a threat to security and competitors for jobs and welfare. The EU should be deeply downsized – in the sense of renationalising policies, strengthening national borders, and

---

[17] P. Corbetta (ed.), *Come cambia il partito di Grillo*, Bologna, Il Mulino, 2017; G. Passarelli and D. Tuorto, *La Lega di Salvini*, Bologna, Il Mulino, 2018.

without excluding the option of restoring the national currency, and leaving the Union (Italexit). The League, as a national populist party, is Eurosceptic and sometimes Europhobic: EU institutions are easy scapegoats for both the crisis of efficiency/ effectiveness and the crisis of legitimacy of European democracies. A deficit of democratic representation surely exists in European governance, and communitarian treaties do put constraints on the autonomous policy choices of member states. But it is an illusion to think that, in the globalising world, separate nation-states have the resources of power necessary to govern the complexity of the present crises and mitigate their effects, whereas they can deepen cleavages and stir new infra-European conflicts, with the risk of following a path already tragically traveled in European history.

The second component of Salvini's League's ideology is economic neo-liberalism with the key corollary of tax reduction. It implies a conflict with the FSM's propensity for state interventionism. It also contradicts the previous, anti-EU component, since the single market is a basic feature of the European Union. The third component, moral and religious conservatism, is more controversial: on the one hand, Salvini proclaims himself a Christian, and his party supports conservative positions on civil liberties matters, like abortion, same-sex marriages, and advance healthcare directive; on the other, the League strongly opposes Pope Francis' attitude toward immigrants. It is a conservative religious position close to that of the Evangelical Protestant and Pentecostal churches, a brand of Protestantism that plaid a very important role in the victory of Donald Trump in the US and Jair Bolsonaro in Brazil. The top programme priorities of the League – included in the "government contract" with the FSM – mostly concern the first two components: a) securitisation and anti-immigration and b) tax reduction and fiscal benefits (like workers' earlier retirement). Except for the last issue, i.e., the dismantling of the Monti-Fornero pension reform, these are not the top priorities of the FSM; this is not a surprise since voters' attitudes and social characteristics strongly influence programme priorities. In today's electoral tactics, populist party leaders, even more than their competitors, look more like party followers, in the sense that they pay feverish attention to the short-term, volatile moods of the electorate. The core of the League electorate was traditionally made of self-employed workers, artisans, small entrepreneurs, residents in small and medium-sized towns of the most economically developed regions of the country. However, the recent huge vote increase is due to the outreach towards other social groups by building on the fact that security is a general, transversal, interclass issue. Currently, the League is still a Northern party (first party with 30% of the vote in Veneto and Lombardy, and well ahead of Forza Italia in Piedmont), but has already made big progress in Central Italy and is growing in the Mezzogiorno as well (in fact, it is here that one can found a clear correlation between immigrants' presence and the vote for the League). The League is a nationalist, but not yet a national, party[18], since it is by far the first party in the North but much behind the FSM in the South. The analysis of electoral flows shows that the traditional electorate of the League in the strongholds of North-East is increased not only by former Berlusconi's supporters (who are sociologically rather similar and account for about one third) but also by people who abstained in the past and by former FSM voters. The key difference between the two types of populism is, therefore, a growing geographical polarisation: the League is strong in the North and the FSM in the South.

The Five Star Movement is a manifestation of populist politics, only moderately nationalist. It is a movement-party[19] and, more specifically, the outcome of a recombination of grassroots single-issue movements, born on the initiative of a comedian, Beppe Grillo, who was able to express the growing sentiment against the privileges of the political "caste" and the widespread demand for moralising political life and renovating democratic

---

[18] G. Passarelli and D. Tuorto (2018).
[19] D. Della Porta, J. Fernandez, H. Kpouki, and L. Mosca, *Movement Parties Against Austerity*, Malden, Polity Press, 2017.

practices. After a "phase zero", in which local grassroots lists certified by Grillo were presented in local elections (January 2008), the FSM went through three phases[20]: in the first, from its foundation upon the initiative of Grillo in October 2009 to 2013 national election, it kept an informal, movement-like character, with constant interactions on the web between the leader and a small, but growing, number of activists. With the entrance of the first movement representatives in local assemblies, more traditional tactics like mass rallies were added to the use of the web; the movement started to institutionalise, although keeping its self-definition of horizontal association (with such slogans as "one is worth one", "non-movement", "non-statute", or using the word "speaker" instead of president or secretary), in order to stress its diversity from traditional parties. The second phase started with the decision to participate in the 2013 national election. New problems had to be addressed: first, the need to outline a government programme (Grillo's "20 points to get out of the dark"– which included the so-called "reddito di cittadinanza" (basic income guarantee), measures for SM firms, improvements of public health and public schools, anti-corruption law, the abolition of public financing for parties, the introduction of the proactive referendum – beyond other issues raised in mass rallies (like a referendum on leaving the EU and the euro and tax reduction measures); second, the need to define more precise criteria for selecting candidates (through web voting in the so-called "parlamentarie", which were at first reserved to those who had previously been elected in local assemblies). The outcomes of these innovations were a hybrid, party/movement organisational structure, the emergence of new leaders, and some downsising of Grillo's – until then – one-man leadership. The success of the FSM was large and quick: it reached 25.5% in the Chamber (almost equal to the Democratic Party that got most of the vote

---

[20] R. Biorcio and P. Natale, *Il Movimento 5 Stelle dalla protesta al governo*, Milano, Mimesis, 2018.

of Italians abroad). The success had been anticipated in the municipal election in Parma (May 2012) and in the regional election in Sicily (October 2012). After the sharp decline in 2014 European Parliament election (when many PD voters who had shifted to the FSM went back to Matteo Renzi's PD that won with 40% of the vote), the growth resumed with the victories in the municipal elections in Rome, Turin, and other cities, paving the way for the nation-wide success of March 2018.

The third phase initiated in the 2018 election campaign and was very successful, making the FSM the relative majority party in both chambers. The process of institutionalisation moved on, with the election of Luigi Di Maio as both political leader and candidate Prime Minister, the direct selection of several candidates by the party leadership, and the presentation of the ministers' list including outside experts. Grillo kept for himself the role of guarantor, while the new party statute gives a key role to the Rousseau platform – the web platform where a large part of the FSM political activity takes place, from the registration of new members to the selection of candidates, from web "direct democracy" consultation to communication and accountability by elected MPs (who must finance the platform with 300 euros a month). Some journalists exposed as unclear the links between the Rousseau platform and the Casaleggio Associates – of which Davide Casaleggio (the son of Gianroberto, friend and co-initiator of the movement with Grillo) is President, CEO, and treasurer. Inroads made by hackers into the platform has prompted the Data Protection Authority to make checks of its safety.

In a few years, the FSM greatly broadened its electoral base: the early activists and sympathysers were newcomers – who found in the movement for the first time an opportunity for political participation – and disappointed leftist voters. With the leap forward of 2012, these two groups were joined by "rational" voters – who saw in the FSM the only force that could transform Italy's political life –, "emotional" voters who despised the caste, and former PD voters who had been disappointed by Matteo Renzi's first attempt to change the party (defeated by Pierluigi Bersani in the party primaries for party secretary) and had a significant impact on the outcome of the 2013 election by shifting their preferences in the last week before the polls. The further growth in consensus in the 2018 general election is largely due to voters who greatly appreciated the promise of implementing the basic income guarantee (the so-callled "citizenship income") mostly in the South, compared to a moderate increase in Central Italy and a slight decline in Northeast Italy. The resulting key change with regard to 2013 is the growing meridionalisation of the party. The analysis of electoral flows shows that almost ¾ of those who voted the FSM in 2013 confirmed their choice, while the increase came from former centre-left voters (mostly in Central Italy) and former centre-right voters and previously non voting people (mostly in the Mezzogiorno). The 2018 FSM electorate was made for 59% of voters who confirmed their 2013 choice, for 14% of non voters, for 18% of former centre-left voters (14% PD and 2% each Monti's party and the radical left), for 9% of former centre-right voters (7% Forza Italia and 1% each Lega and Fratelli d'Italia).

The growth of the party added new claims and implied a partial reset of programme priorities, adapting them to the demands of different segments of the electorate (and to the specific type of election), a tactic which works well for an opposition party but much less so for a government party (the more so in a coalition with another party having different priorities). Among Grillo's "20 points to get out of the dark", the basic income guarantee has become the top priority; other original proposals like an anti-corruption law, the reduction of privileges for the political class, tax reduction, and measures for SM firms were kept, while others like more funds for public health and public education were downgraded, and the referendum on Italexit was confined to Grillo's shows.

Given the differences between the FSM and the League, the formation of the new government was long and difficult but looked like the only option, since neither the centre-right coalition nor the centre-left coalition had the majority, and the PD rejected an FSM proposal to form a coalition. After three months, an agreement was finally reached by the two winning parties, despite their ideological differences. However, two minorities do not make necessarily a majority and can hardly guarantee a stable government with a coherent programme.

One might wonder on which basis this coalition is built and how long will it last. The government coalition is strengthened by the two parties' common will to remain in power long enough to build a new power system in the many government agencies, state-controlled firms, and political bodies that are led by government nominees. The election of the presidents of the lower and upper chamber and many parliament committees before and after the forming of the coalition, the partition of posts among party supporters, and the distribution of benefits to party clients, show that the League and the FSM are capable of making compromises. Moreover, each party tries not to interfere with the other's declared programme priorities and seems willing to divide the scarce public resources needed to implement them. Conflicts appear, however, inevitable and are already taking place on issues like the new security law and the reform of criminal proceedings. Also, their strategies for achieving economic growth diverge: for the FSM, the driver is the domestic demand that should be boosted by the basic income guarantee, for the League, the driver is tax-free corporate investment in innovation and infrastructures. Hence the conflicts on implementing industrial projects like the control of Taranto's Ilva by Arcelor Mittal and the Trans-Adriatic Pipeline (TAP), and on financing infrastructures like the high-speed railways between Turin and Lyon and Brescia and Venice, or the third railway crossing between Genoa and Milan.

Divergent opinions and conflicts between the two partners make it hard to predict how long the government will last, if until the European election or after. What it is not hard to forecast is that the coalition between two populist parties with different priorities implies a much heavier burden for the public budget than it would have been if one of the two had reached a parliamentary majority alone. As I already remarked, each party tries not to undercut the achievement of the other's electoral goals, with the result of adding expenditure to expenditure (basic income guarantee and early retirement) and of reducing the fiscal income (flat tax). The collision course with the European governance (that accuses Italy to violate agreed budget rules), the growing risk of isolation of Italy in the EU and, even more worrisome, the negative reaction of the financial markets appear inevitable. One could, however, argue that the policy choices of the yellow-green government are not new, since also in the past quite different policy priorities had been jointly pursued. The political proposal actually reminds us those of past DC-led governments (although in a quite different political context).

The "government contract" between the FSM and the League is, in this respect, a mix of old and new. Old is the double strategy of tax reduction and fiscal leniency (flat tax, tax amnesty) for those voters who belong to the better-off social groups and/or live in the richer parts of the country (most of the North), on the one hand, and patronage welfarism with significant state aid for those voters who belong to the worse-off social groups and/or live in the poorer parts of the country like vast areas in the Mezzogiorno, on the other. This dual strategy was a key component of the consensus organisation of the Christian Democratic Party and, to a lesser extent, of its government partners (PSI, PSDI, PLI) in the 1970s and 1980s. This strategy clearly had a cost, i.e., the huge increase in the public debt, but was for many years an effective and viable strategy, until the Maastricht parameters of fiscal austerity and the "Clean hands" investigation – exposing corrupted lobbying and party clientelism – forced government parties to give it up (at least temporarily). In a country like Italy, where many citizens claim the right to get help from the state but forget their civic duties such as respecting the law and paying taxes, the combination of poorly regulated private business and generous state assistance has often been an effective way to win consensus, although it has hardly provided good governance.

The government contract underwritten by the FSM and the League contains election promises which remind of the double strategy outlined above: "fiscal peace" – as it is called the wide tax amnesty proposed by the government – and "flat tax" – that tends to favour high- and middle-income groups – will be more welcomed by League supporters, which include many autonomous workers, small businessmen, and public bonds holders, whereas the basic income guarantee will mostly be welcomed by the M5S electorate, which includes large numbers of unemployed and underemployed. The social divide is also a territorial divide, since the League – although extending its reach, has still its electoral strongholds in the North, while the FSM is significantly more voted by those living in the South. However, the attempt to rehash the old compromise – which was at the core of Christian Democrats' electoral consensus in the "First Republic"– raises a two-fold problem: first, these promises are not made by a single party but by two different parties which share government power in a complex and difficult relationship of competitive cooperation. The Christian Democratic Party could manage the North/South dualism through a complex system of mediation, intermediation, compromise, checks and balances, between different "currents" and regional bosses, who were united by the common goal of keeping their party in power. The present yellow-green coalition, on the other hand, has an inherent contradiction which can explode if certain conditions take place, as I argued above.

The second problem is that the same factors that contributed to ending Christian Democracy-led governments in the "First Republic" – i.e., EU constraints on member states' monetary and fiscal policies (the Maastricht parameters) and the reactions of globally interconnected financial markets which did not allow this type of free-wheel public finance – are still present. Italy is exposed to EU infringement proceedings for disregarding European regulations, and the cost of refinancing the debt is rising due to the declining trust of financial investors. The

FSM and the League face the problem of rising expenditures if they want to deliver what they promised during the electoral campaign. All opposition parties face it once they get to power, but the problem is even more acute for populist parties since they run campaigns which exaggerate promises and simplify the ways to fulfill them in very short time (such as ending poverty in a few months with a single law, i.e., the "citizenship income"); and it is even more acute in Italy now, since there are two populist parties in power, not just one, each striving to implement its own set of priorities. After the government decision to raise to 2.4% the deficit/GDP ratio for the next three fiscal years in 2019 budget law, the FSM's ministers celebrated it as a victory, arguing that the resources needed to implement programme priorities had to be found despite EU "unreasonable" budgetary constraints, because those priorities are the reasons why voters chose their party. To experts – like the INPS president Tito Boeri or former spending review commissioner Carlo Cottarelli – who warned that the financial burden resulting from basic income guarantee, pension law reform, and flat tax would be too high for a country with such a huge public debt, the leader of the League answered by inviting them to stop criticising and forming instead their own parties. The reaction of financial markets (the rising spread between Italian and German bonds, Italian banks' losses in the stock exchange, the downward revision of Italy's GDP, the downgrading of Italy sovereign debt by rating agencies) prompted a limited change of the budget law (a lower public deficit increase in 2020 and 2021) but, on the whole, the Italian government is keeping his decision, while EU institutions are making clear that violations of the common rules cannot be accepted. Despite goodwill declarations from both sides that an agreement will be finally reached, no significant changes in the budget law are likely to take place unless the economic situation worsens very much. If this is the case, the two populist parties will likely resort to the well-known tactics of putting the blame on others; they will argue that the government did its best but was prevented from doing what it

wanted by external powers, such as the unreasonable EU political elites and wicked global financial elites, all acting against the
interests of Italian people. If, on the other hand, the deterioration of Italy's economic situation is kept within tolerable limits,
the government parties will celebrate victory over an impotent
EU. In both cases, the national-populist campaign against the
EU in the European Parliament election will be strengthened,
although blame-shifting and scapegoating work only up to a
certain point.

From the analogy with the Christian Democracy-led government of the "First Republic", one should not draw, however,
the impression that the FSM and the League are not innovat-
ing Italian politics as instances of neo-populism, coupled in the
case of the League with neo-nationalism. Several elements justify defining them populist parties and help explain why they
won the election. First, the illiberal character of populist rhetoric that manifests itself in many statements; just to mention a
few, the frequent reference to Art.1 of the Italian Constitution
("Sovereignty belongs to the people"), forgetting to mention
its second part ("that exercises it in the forms and within the
boundaries set by the Constitution"); the post-election post-
ers celebrating the victory of the League that state "the People
won", thus drawing a sharp line between "us"– the good citizens
who support the party – and all others, who are not considered part of the political community. Second, attacks directed
at institutions that should ensure that checks and balances remain in place, and that are key components of a liberal democracy: in the FSM case, the party attacked Italy's President
when he refused to agree on the nomination of Paolo Savona,
a Eurosceptic minister; in case of the League, the party criticised judges arguing that judges have not been elected and
should not interfere with those who represent the will of the
people; both parties threatened to cut funds to the press because is too critical of the government. Third, the skillful use of
social media (Facebook, Twitter, Instagram) and the tendency
to react immediately to dramatic events – like the collapse of

the Genoa bridge – identifying scapegoats and fostering blame shifting on past governments, to disseminate misleading news and data (like the ones on the financial contribution of Italy to the EU), to make party leaders familiar figures by showing their private lives. This use of new media has successfully changed the political discourse and reframed political debates. Fourth, the ability to perceive the frustrations and resentments of many citizens at the local level, in urban peripheries, small towns, the countryside, and politically exploit them. Fifth (for the FSM), a strong inclination toward "web democracy" through permanent online consultations between elected representatives and followers. By reverse, distinctive populist characteristics like anti-technocratic feelings have been softly downgraded because the transition from anti-elite opposition to government requires to rely on technocrats and take "pragmatic" decisions about previously ideologically loaded issues, even at the price of stirring criticism and protest among supporters.

The key problem of the League is how to become a national party, increasing consensus outside its traditional strongholds; to this purpose, it will likely emphasise a nationalist and Eurosceptic anti-EU discourse. The key problem of the FSM is the institutionalisation of the movement, the transition from a loose federation of territorial and web communities into a party organisation, with the related problems of the succession to Grillo's leadership and the definition of a model of society that could replace the present heterogeneous set of "post-ideological" narratives. The inherent difficulties of those problems are aggravated for both parties by the fact that solutions must be pursued in the context of fierce competition within the odd couple in government.

National Populism and the Future of the EU

Italy is a special case of national populism in today's Europe. However, the diffusion of both nationalism and populism goes well beyond Italy. The convergence of nationalist ideology and populist rhetoric and the rise of national-populist leaders, movements, and parties is the main symptom of the crisis of democratic representation in contemporary Europe and the major challenge that the European Union faces since its birth, a challenge that can be effectively countered only by developing the political project of a truly democratic supranational union[21]. The risk exists that the rationalising power of parties and institutions might be severely reduced by the ebbs and flows of volatile and ephemeral political moods, thus triggering a vicious circle between weak and short-sighted governments and protest populist movements without perspectives, right at the time when the need for legitimate and efficient governments, able to face a series of intertwined crises (low economic growth, high unemployment, massive migration, terrorism) is stronger than ever. The supporters of populist anti-EU parties criticise real pathologies of democratic life and sincerely wish to cure them, but their conception of democracy is often rudimental and incomplete and fosters the rise of intolerant, plebiscitarian leaders who, once in power, prove incapable of governing complexity.

National populism can provide an answer, although limited, to the legitimacy crisis of contemporary democracies insofar as it offers an identity basis to many globalisation losers, who pinpoint transnational elites and the EU bureaucracy and technocracy as the root of all their problems of unemployment, precariousness, declining income, and generalised insecurity. But their strategy for restoring full national sovereignty and renationalising policy-making cannot respond effectively to the interrelated crises of unequal development, poverty, terrorism, and war because the constraints on sovereignty imposed by globalisation do not disappear but are, on the contrary, even stronger and more pervasive for political entities that are smaller and weaker than a supranational union.

The coming election of May 2019, the first after Brexit, will likely bring significant changes in European politics. For the

---

[21] A. Martinelli (2016).

first time, the key issue will be the future of the Union and its institutional reform; and the key confrontation will be between those who support a deeper political integration and those who are in favour of restoring national sovereignty. A simulation of the 2019 outcome on the basis of the results in recent national elections in member countries shows that votes for national-populist parties will increase but not to the point of reaching a majority in parliament; these parties could, however, get enough votes to form a blocking minority, since most decisions – beyond those requiring unanimity – are taken by a qualified majority vote, including the election of the Commission President. In his 2018 State of the Union speech, Jean Claude Juncker urged each major party federations to renew their decision to nominate their own candidate (*Spitzenkandidat*) for Commission President and select the one who gets more votes. The pro-EU coalition that elected him four years ago – Christian-Democrats, Socialists, and Liberals – only had 45 votes more than necessary. The two Eurosceptic groups in the EP can count now on 45 EFDD (Europe of Freedom and Direct Democracy) and 35 of ENF (Europe of Nations and Freedom) MPs, but this time the populist wave will be stronger. If the 45 votes more than the needed majority vanish due to the increase of votes for populist Eurosceptic parties, new scenarios open up: either a stalemate in EU politics or a new enlarged coalition, including the Greens.

If one takes into account not only the relations of force among party federations but also their internal dynamics, it is worth noting the efforts of the EPP (European's People Party) and ALDE (Alliance of Liberals and Democrats for Europe) to keep their Eurosceptic components challenging their mainstream pro-EU position, like Orban in the EPP and, to a lesser extent, the German FDP (Free Democratic Party) in ALDE. At the same time, keeping the unity of the federation runs the risk of shifting the axis of these parties to the right on key policy choices, first of all, migration and borders policies. This intention was clearly stated by CSU's (Christian Social Union) Manfred

Weber, the President of the European People's Party group in the EP, who has been nominated as the official candidate for the top Commission job at the EPP congress in November 2018 despite his party decline in the last Bavarian election. In a September 2018 interview, Weber described himself as a "bridge builder" and called on conservatives to "listen" to populist leaders and "find compromises" in order to avoid another Brexit; but he added that the "identity question" would dominate the electoral campaign and that a European identity and way of life does exist, which includes secular values, democracy, the rule of law, and press freedom. The internal dynamics of the EPP is relevant for the future of the EU, a complex game that will be influenced by the already ongoing competition for replacing Angela Merkel as CDU (Christian Democratic Union) leader in 2021. A first test of this conflict was the yes vote of the European Parliament on the motion calling for triggering Article 7 against Hungary over the alleged rule of law breaches; even though Orban's Fidesz party is still part of the EPP family, the internal struggle in the EPP is far from over.

Similar tensions and struggles are taking place, in various ways, within the other major EU party federations in what will be the most crucial election since the birth of the EU. The cleavage between pro-EU and anti-EU parties is at the core of the campaign for the 2019 European Parliament, a fact that proves the exceptional foresight of the Manifesto that Eugenio Colorni, Ernesto Rossi, and Altiero Spinelli wrote in confinement on the island of Ventotene, during the darkest hour of the second World war:

> [...] the dividing line between progressive and reactionary parties no longer coincides with the formal lines indicating a more or less advanced democracy, a more or less developed form of socialism, but rather with a very new, substantial line: on one side are those who see the old objective of struggle, in other words the conquest of national political power, and who will, albeit involuntarily, play into the hands of the reactionary forces, by allowing the incandescent lava of popular passions to set in the old molds with past absurdities resurfacing, while on the other

side are those who see their main duty as the creation of a solid international state, who will direct popular forces towards this goal, and who, even if they gain national power, will use it above all as an instrument to bring about international unity.

2. National-Populism in Trump's First Year of Presidency

Eliza Tanner Hawkins, Kirk A. Hawkins

Commentators and pundits are fond of pointing out that President Donald Trump is unlike any US president they have known. Well into his second year as President, his actions continue to be unpredictable, even for his own staff. He governs via Twitter. He delights in upsetting political conventions and thrives on chaos. In the international realm, former allies are often treated as enemies and historic foes may get a warm welcome. Despite the constant political turmoil surrounding the US presidency and the inability to predict Trump's daily actions, we are able to say a few things relating to national populism in the United States. This chapter looks at how nationalism is intertwined with populism in the United States. It argues that although Trump remains a populist and continues to promote an "America first" ideology, the US political system creates an environment where the possible outcome differs from what we see in Central and Eastern Europe, where populists enjoy increasing strength and are undermining core institutions of liberal democracy. Instead, it is closer to populism in the relatively affluent parts of Western Europe, where support for populists challenges democracy, but without destroying its foundations.

We first present data on Trump as a nationalist populist, highlighting the consistency in his rhetoric and policies since the campaign. We then look at the broadening or shrinking of his coalition, noting especially the changes in the Republican

Party and the polarisation that have accompanied his entering office. Since it is impossible to talk about Trump without
taking into account his political style, we briefly look at his
rhetoric and then his actual achievements at implementing his
nationalist populist vision. Finally we look at his limited impact
on America's democratic institutions and conclude with a few
thoughts about what the future may hold for Trumpism.

Trump's Persistent Nationalist Populism

An immediate question is whether Trump is still (or ever was) a
nationalist populist. To understand this, we must consider two
features of Trump: his populism and his nationalism.

Elsewhere we have argued that Trump was a populist in the
2016 campaign, albeit in a limited way that says much about
his political outlook[1]. By "populist" we mean that he frames
politics as a struggle between the will of the common people
and an evil, conspiring elite; this kind of discourse stands in
opposition to a pluralist one in which political opponents are
not demonised, and disagreement and compromise are seen as
valued and natural features of democracy. To measure Trump's
populism in the campaign, we performed a textual analysis of
his speeches and debates, roughly two per month; we also studied similar texts for the other candidates. We found that Trump
was often populist, but only inconsistently. While he consistently spoke out against an "establishment" of Washington
insiders, global financiers, and liberal Democrats, in many of
his speeches and most of his debates, he omitted references to
the virtues of the common people and celebrated himself and
his team. Tellingly, his most clearly populist speeches (those in
which he did reference groups such as "the American people")
were those in which he used a teleprompter, i.e., those prepared

---

[1] K.A. Hawkins, R. Dudley, and W. Jie (Fred) Tan, "Made in US: Populism
Beyond Europe", in A. Martinelli (ed.), *Populism on the Rise, Democracies Under
Challenge?*, Milan, Epoké-ISPI, 2016.

with the help of speechwriters. Thus, Trump himself only seems to express an incomplete form of populism that lacks a belief in popular sovereignty.

In the campaign, Trump could also be considered a nationalist, in the sense used in this volume. Ideologically speaking, he belonged to what other political scientists define as radical right populism: a combination of populism with nativism and support for traditional social values[2]. As detailed in an earlier ISPI publication[3], Trump campaigned on a platform of restraining immigration by building a border wall and strengthening laws and personnel for border control; revisiting international trade agreements to benefit national producers and bring jobs back to America; improved funding for the nation's military and for responding forcefully to crime at home; active opposition to abortion access and LGBT rights; and favouritism towards certain religious groups, especially evangelical Christians.

This pattern of nationalism and populism persisted during his first couple of years in office. To begin with, a fully developed form of populist discourse clearly persists in some of his speeches, but inconsistently. To measure this, we conducted another textual analysis, this time of six speeches from his first year in office, with two speeches from each of three categories we have used elsewhere to rank government chief executives in office, namely, famous, international, and ribbon-cutting speeches. The results are in Table 1.

---

[2] C. Mudde, *Populist Radical Right Parties in Europe.* Cambridge, Cambridge University Press, 2007.

[3] K.A. Hawkins, R. Dudley, and W. Jie (Fred) Tan (2016).

Tab. 1 - Trump's populist rhetoric
during his first year (scale 0-2)

Speech	Date	Score
Inaugural	20 Jan 2017	1.55
Joint Address to Congress	28 Feb 2017	0.80
Arab Islamic American Summit in Saudi Arabia	21 May 2017	0.40
Congressional Picnic	22 Jun 2017	0.00
People of Poland	6 Jul 2017	0.90
Mississippi Civil Rights Museum	9 Dec 2017	0.35
Average		0.67

Interestingly, we find that Trump has about the same average level of populism as in his campaign (roughly 0.7 on a scale of 0 to 2) and shows much of the same variability in language. Sometimes, as in his inaugural address, he speaks a strong form of populism that talks about "the just and reasonable demands of a righteous public" ignored and taken advantage of by "a small group in our nation's Capital"[4]. At other times, however, there is little if any populism and his speeches come across as typical ceremonial speeches with a more pluralistic, if patriotic feel, as in his address to the 2017 Arab American Summit in Saudi Arabia, where he states "We must practice tolerance and respect for each other once again"[5], or in a speech at the dedication of the Mississippi Civil Rights Museum in December, where he declares "We want our country to be a place where every child, from every background, can grow up free from fear, innocent of hatred, and surrounded by love, opportunity, and

---

[4] "The Inaugural Address", The White House, 20 January 2017.
[5] "President Trump's Speech to the Arab Islamic American Summit", The White House, 21 May 2017.

hope"[6]. Because all of these latest speeches involve teleprompters and, we presume, speechwriters, our explanation is that he draws from an array of speechwriters. Some are individuals such as Steve Miller, a long-time advisor from the campaign who is known for his own populist sensibilities, while others such as his son-in-law Jared Kushner, are known for their moderate views and attempts to temper the President's rhetoric[7].

Likewise, Trump's nationalist talk and positions have also persisted in office. This is easily seen in his speeches and communications (which is usually his Twitter feed). He constantly stresses patriotism and ideas of returning the United States to its former greatness. For example, during a typical week in May-June 2018, he used phrases such as "Make America Great Again", "a true American Patriot the likes of which we rarely see in our modern day world", and "We love our country. We want to keep our country great". Two different topics illustrate how Trump's nationalism continues during his time in office. The first topic has to do with the controversy surrounding protests by National Football League (NFL) players over the deaths of unarmed black men at the hands of police officers. NFL players began to kneel in protest, instead of stand, when the US National Anthem was played at the beginning of football games. Trump severely criticised this as unpatriotic and in May 2018, the governing body of the NFL mandated that the players stand for the National Anthem or remain in the locker rooms. After this decision, Trump's tweeted "We will proudly be playing the National Anthem and other wonderful music celebrating our Country today" and "Staying in the Locker Room for the playing of our National Anthem is as disrespectful to our country as kneeling. Sorry!". As part of his nationalist talk, he promotes an idea of patriotism that is closely aligned with the far right, including such things as reverence and respect for symbols of America like the flag.

---

[6] "Remarks by President Trump at the Opening of the Mississippi Civil Rights Museum", The White House, 9 December 2017.

[7] L. Mascaro, "Trump Speechwriter Stephen Miller, a Santa Monica High Grad, Pens Address for President's Middle East Visit", *Los Angeles Times*, 19 May 2017.

Trade is another area where Trump's speech continues to show his nationalism. For example, on June 4, 2018, he wrote, "Farmers have not been doing well for 15 years. Mexico, Canada, China and others have treated them unfairly. By the time I finish trade talks, that will change. Big trade barriers against US farmers, and other businesses, will finally be broken. Massive trade deficits no longer!". A few days previous, he wrote, "When you're almost 800 Billion Dollars a year down on Trade, you can't lose a Trade War! The US has been ripped off by other countries for years on Trade, time to get smart!". Setting aside the truth or fallacy of his claims, what we see throughout Trump's communication is an emphasis on putting first the interests of various sectors in America (such as farmers or coal workers) over ideas of international cooperation or trade agreements. He is extremely consistent in repeating and promoting the idea of "America First". Nor has he moderated in his actual rhetoric and communication[8].

These are important findings, because some scholars analysing nationalist populist parties in Europe have suggested that populists should adopt a more moderate discourse once in office[9]. According to this view, as populists are forced into the difficult challenge of governing, especially under the hard choices imposed by finite resources in a globalised economy, not to mention the oft-competing interests of their constituents, populists will compromise on some of their extravagant campaign promises and adopt a softer rhetoric that can build greater support for their government.

Trump shows that the moderation of populism in office is more of an open question. While some populist parties in Western Europe may moderate, parties in Latin America have not historically done so (think of the persistent radicalism of Juan

---

[8] For complete transcripts of Trump's communication see https://factba.se/trump and http://www.trumptwitterarchive.com/

[9] P. Taggart and A. Szczerbiak, "Coming in from the Cold? Euroscepticism, Government Participation and Party Positions on Europe", *JCMS: Journal of Common Market Studies*, vol. 51, no. 1, 2013, pp. 17-37.

Domingo Perón in Argentina or Hugo Chávez in Venezuela), and it is not true of Trump or many of his Republican supporters in Congress during his first two years in office. While there is still considerable tension in the party between populist radicals and moderates, the party leadership has generally found itself following Trump's lead rather than tempering his discourse and policy positions. To be clear, Trump was never as consistently or as loudly populist as other well-known figures, including a few in the US today such as Bernie Sanders. But he has maintained essentially the same kind of nationalist populist rhetoric as he did during the campaign.

Support, or Lack Thereof, for Trump's Goals/ Trump's Constant Coalition

Given Trump's continuing nationalist populist rhetoric, how has his coalition shifted, and do we see a broadening consensus around his policies? National populists in countries such as Hungary and Turkey have been able to maintain or even expand a broad electoral mandate once in office, despite radicalising their rhetoric, while populists in Western Europe and other advanced industrial democracies have struggled to do so.

To answer this, we must first point out that Trump came to office without much of a consensus. Although his Electoral College vote was high, this was because the Republican vote was spread out across more states, while the Democratic vote for Hilary Clinton was concentrated in urban centres of the East and West Coasts. In fact, Trump's share of the popular vote (46%) was below that of Hillary Clinton (48%). Moreover, Trump's support was fairly equivocal: while many voters supported him because of his nationalist positions and populist sentiment, others supported him out of opposition to Clinton and felt reservations about his character. Thus, it is somewhat misleading to think of Trump as broadening or shrinking his electoral mandate since he never really had one.

That said, since coming to office, Trump has not really expanded his overall level of support, although he has reinforced
his backing among Republican voters, who now provide him
with an important voter base. And, while he has not really
changed the overall spread of voters' ideology or partisanship
in the US, his rhetoric and issue positions have contributed to
long-term polarising trends in US politics.

Overall support for Trump has fluctuated somewhat across
his first two years but remains modest, declining from around
45% levels of job approval at the start of his term to a low of
around 35% at the end of 2017, and rebounding slightly to
above 40% at the time of this writing in mid-2018[10]. This overall modest level hides a high level of partisanship. Self-declared
Republicans (about 25% of the electorate) overwhelmingly have
a high opinion of the job the President is doing. Public opinion
polls consistently show almost 90% approval ratings for Trump
among Republicans, versus around 35% among independents
and 5-10% among Democrats[11]. To be clear, this kind of partisanship is not unusual for presidents towards the end of their
terms, especially in recent years of increasing polarisation, but
it is unusual at the start of the term, when presidents-elect normally enjoy a honeymoon of relatively broad support.

Who is in Trump's coalition? While it has shrunk slightly since
winning office, his voters are disproportionately white, male (especially among crossover Democrat voters), older (65+ years),
Protestant (especially Evangelical), less educated, blue-collar
workers or serving in the military, and/or rural. These patterns
largely correspond to Republican/conservative voting in recent years, although Trump's election marked at least a small
shift of low-skilled blue-collar workers in the Midwest away
from the Democratic Party. More important, they are the same
groups that supported him most strongly in the election – the

---

[10] "Polls: President Trump Job Approval", Realclearpolitics.com, 14 June 2018;
N. Silver, "How Popular Is Donald Trump?", *FiveThirtyEight*, 14 June 2018.
[11]"Presidential Approval Ratings - Donald Trump", Gallup.com, 2018.

coalition is essentially unchanged[12]. This coalition is typical of radical-right parties across other wealthy democracies, where the nationalist populist message appeals largely to so-called "losers of globalisation", both in its cultural and economic forms.

Many commentators are concerned that Trump is polarising the electorate, a phenomenon that might serve to strengthen his coalition by forcing independents partisans and ideological moderates to choose sides (and opt for Trump). In fact, Trump does seem to be deepening some kinds of polarisation of the US electorate, especially what political scientists call partisan sorting and affective polarisation. The former is when voters move to parties that better represent their personal ideological or issue stances, but without necessarily changing those stances[13]. The latter refers to the dislike that partisans feel for their opponents – for example, whether they would be willing to live near each other or marry into each other's families[14].

Studies from the election show heightened levels of these types of polarisation. For example, there is a continued trend towards ideological homogeneity among Trump's partisan supporters and greater ideological distance with supporters of the opposite party. Those who identify as Republican especially agree on cultural issues that in European are known as the GAL-TAN divide: Green/Alternative/Libertarian vs. Traditional/Authoritarianism/Nationalist beliefs[15]. Likewise, voters in the election show the highest levels of dislike for voters and candidates of the opposite party in several decades[16].

---

[12] R. Florida, "Approval of Trump Maps Onto a Starkly Divided U.S.", *CityLab*, 15 February 2018; K. Yourish and B. Migliozzi, "A Year Later, Trump Is Less Popular Across Voting Blocs. See by How Much", *The New York Times*, 11 January 2018.

[13] M. Levendusky, *The Partisan Sort: How Liberals Became Democrats and Conservatives Became Republicans*, Chicago, University of Chicago Press, 2009.

[14] S. Iyengar, G. Sood, and Y. Lelkes, "Affect, Not Ideology: A Social Identity Perspective on Polarization", *Public Opinion Quarterly*, vol. 76, no. 3, 2012, pp. 405-31.

[15] L.M. Bartels, *Partisanship in the Trump Era*, Working Paper, Centre for the Study of Democratic Institutions, Nashville, Vanderbilt University, 2018.

[16] S. Iyengar and M. Krupenkin, "The Strengthening of Partisan Affect", *Political*

However, claims about increasing polarisation require two major caveats. First, it is incorrect to blame it on the emergence of a nationalist populist candidate – the trend predates Trump. US political scientists have been describing growing partisan polarisation for years, a process that seems to have its origins in the divide over social issues that first emerged in the late 1960s[17]. While populism has polarising effects, the 2016 election is clearly a case where populism was preceded by or even facilitated by polarisation. This is not true in every country – one thinks here of Venezuela in the late 1990s, when there was a high level of consensus about the basic symptoms of the failures of the political system before Chávez was elected, and where most forms of polarisation appeared after the election[18]. Furthermore, the studies just mentioned show that trends in the US have continued to worsen. But polarisation clearly preceded the 2016 US campaign and is part of a long-term process.

Second, and perhaps more importantly, polarisation in the US consists primarily of partisan sorting and affective polarisation, not a radical shift in the underlying distribution of citizens' attitudes about issues and ideology[19]. The aggregate distribution of voter positions on key issues – including those that Trump ran on, such as immigration – has not shifted all that much, and most of these distributions remain unimodal, not bimodal. For example, attitudes towards immigration have remained largely unchanged for the past four years, and over the past two decades they have actually grown more favourable to immigrants. Whereas in 2002 only 7-8% of Americans felt that immigration should increase, today nearly 25% of voters feel that immigration should increase; the number of those who

Psychology, vol. 39, S1, 2018, pp. 201-18.

[17] A. Abramowitz, *The Disappearing Centre: Engaged Citizens, Polarization, and American Democracy*, New Haven, CT, Yale University Press, 2010.

[18] S. Handlin, *State Crisis in Fragile Democracies: Polarization and Political Regimes in South America*, Cambridge, Cambridge University Press, 2017.

[19] Y. Lelkes, "Mass Polarization: Manifestations and Measurements", Public Opinion Quarterly, vol. 80, S1, 2016, pp. 392-410.

feel immigration should decrease dropped in this same period from 58% to 35%[20]. Likewise, most voters remain ideologically moderate, and a plurality of the electorate are still independent – an all-time high of around 45%[21]. This does not mean that moderate, independent voters prefer to vote for nontraditional parties and independent candidates – they still "lean" towards one party or the other in terms of issue positions and their final vote[22] – but they reject the partisan labels and negative affect that seem to accompany them. Thus, to reemphasise the earlier point, Trump does not have the support of most of the electorate in terms of issues, and many Americans who voted for him on election day (about two-fifths of his electorate) did so for pragmatic reasons, because they preferred him to the alternative. That picture has not changed. Trump has failed to break into these other segments of the electorate, and his most fervent supporters remain limited to those who identify as Republicans.

All of this information about polarisation and the size or issue-basis of Trump's constituency speaks primarily to the nationalist side of appeal, to the issues that divide voters and the parties. But the populist side (belief in the virtue of the common citizen, demonisation of the political establishment) plays a role as well and may help explain Trump's ability to maintain the support of Republican voters. This has puzzled many commentators, who assume that his boastful, abrasive style and often wildly inaccurate statements would undermine his voters' confidence in his leadership skills and his willingness to enact his platform. One fact-checking organisation finds that more than 60% of his checked statements are mostly false or completely false[23]. (This contrasts strongly with former President Barack Obama, who averaged about 76% true or mostly/half

---

[20] "In-Depth: Immigration", Gallup.com, 2018a.
[21] "Presidential Approval Ratings - Donald Trump"…, cit.
[22] B.E. Keith, D.B. Magleby, C.J. Nelson, E.A. Orr, and M.C. Westlye, *The Myth of the Independent Voter*, Berkeley, University of California Press, 1992.
[23] "Donald Trump's File", Politifact.com, 2018.

true statements[24]). The *Washington Post* reported in May 2018 that Trump was now averaging 6.5 false or misleading claims every day, for a total of 3,001 since he was sworn in. This number has been slowly increasing, from 4.9 false or misleading claims a day during his first 100 days in office. Moreover, he will repeat these false or misleading claims. For example, Trump has claimed he passed the biggest tax cut in history (it ranks in 8th place among US federal government tax cuts) at least 72 times[25]. Trump's method of using lies predates his presidency. One former Trump associate reported that Trump said, "You just tell them and they believe it"[26]. It appears that he believes that if he repeats something often enough, at least his core supporters will believe what he says even it has no basis in reality.

Part of the explanation for his continuing support may be that his voters simply refuse to believe any contradictory information, what political psychologists call confirmation bias. An NBC/Survey Monkey poll from April 2018 found that 61% of Americans feel that Trump tells the truth "only some of the time or less". When these numbers were divided along party lines, it showed Democrats (94%) and Independents (76%) felt Trump did not tell the truth. In sharp contrast, 75% of Republicans agreed with the statement that Trump told the truth "all or most of the time"[27].

Yet Trump's carelessness with facts also bolsters his populist appeal. A study attempting to find out why Trump supporters would ignore his false statements looked at the role of the "lying demagogue" (which they define as someone who deliberately tells lies and appeals to non-normative private prejudices)

---

[24] "Barack Obama's File", Politifact.com, 2018a.

[25] G. Kessler, S. Rizzo, and M. Kelly, "Analysis: President Trump Has Made 3,001 False or Misleading Claims so Far", *Washington Post*, 1 May 2018, Fact Checker Analysis, Analysis Interpretation of the news based on evidence, including data, as well as anticipating how events might unfold based on past events.

[26] E. Wemple, "Why Does Trump Lie? Just Ask Billy Bush", *Washington Post* (blog), 29 May 2018.

[27] A. Arenge, J. Lapinski, and A. Tallevi, "Poll: Republicans Who Think Trump Is Untruthful Still Approve of Him", *NBC News*, 2 May 2018.

in politics. A series of experiments showed that people who be-lieved the US political system was suffering a legitimacy crisis saw a candidate who violated norms of truth-telling and ap-pealed to their prejudices as an authentic champion of their interests. So, even though Trump's supporters may recognise his statements as false, they seem to be persuaded by his populist rhetoric and persistent policy positions that he is an "authentic" leader who will support their interests. They see his lies as his way of "challenging the elite establishment"[28].

Beyond the Rhetoric: Delivering Policy

While Trump's rhetoric has allowed him to maintain the persis-tent support of core partisan supporters, it has made legislative action difficult. Thus, nationalist populism under Trump has only partially succeeded at achieving its policy goals. At first this seems extraordinary, given his party's control of both houses of Congress. But nationalist populist rhetoric is a two-edged sword: while uniting core supporters, it alienates the rest of the elec-torate and the politicians who represent them, including in this instance some within his own party. While a number of Trump's co-partisans in Congress feel the pressure of Trump's dedicated supporters in primary elections, they confront a much larger elec-torate in the general election, and this often produces ideologi-cally moderate winners even from within the Republican Party. When the timing of the electoral cycle gives them the opportuni-ty, these moderate co-partisans (more present in the Senate than in the House) speak their mind and vote against the party's radi-cals. Furthermore, the continuing legitimacy of other branches of government and independent agencies means that the president frequently encounters roadblocks to his agenda. The exception is those areas of law that are controlled by executive decree.

---

[28] O. Hahl, K. Minjae, and E.W. Zuckerman Sivan, "The Authentic Appeal of the Lying Demagogue: Proclaiming the Deeper Truth about Political Illegitimacy", *American Sociological Review*, vol. 83, no. 1, 2018, pp. 1-33.

Consider first Trump's overall fulfillment of campaign promises. By some counts, Trump made more than 280 campaign
promises, ranging from constructing a wall between the United
States and Mexico to repealing the Affordable Care Act or
Obamacare. At some point in the campaign, he even promised
the American people, "I will give you everything"[29].

That said, during the campaign he issued a "Contract with
the American Voter" that listed 60 concrete promises he would
achieve during the first 100 days in office (Trump n.d.). Half-
way through his second year, various groups and news organisations are still keeping track of these promises and any action
on them, though they tend to focus on the just the top few. As
of June 2018, the *Washington Post* reported that Trump kept 14
promises, broke 16 promises, launched 15, compromised on 7,
and was stuck on 8[30]. The fact-checking organisation PolitiFact
found 10 promises kept, 7 promises broken, 7 compromised,
33 stalled, and 45 in the works[31]. Other tracking organisations
reported similar mixed results[32].

What areas of policy reform has Trump has succeeded at?
Generally, if the policy change is something he can implement
unilaterally without working with Congress, Trump moves
quickly. Thus, most of his successes have come in the area of
foreign policy, especially if the success depends on a negative
action, i.e., withdrawing from an agreement. For example,
one of Trump's campaign promises was to withdraw from the
2015 Paris Agreement on climate change mitigation. In June
2017, Trump made good on that promise and announced the
US withdrawal, even though a large majority of Americans opposed it[33].

---

[29] E. Stokols, "Unapologetic, Trump Promises to Make America Rich", *Politico*,
26 May 2016.
[30] "The Fact Checker's Guide to 60 Promises by Donald Trump", *Washingtonpost.
com*, 30 April 2018.
[31] "Trump-O-Meter: Tracking Trump's Campaign Promises", Politifact.com, 2018.
[32] B. Jackson, "Trump's Numbers", FactCheck.org (blog), 19 January 2018.
[33] "Do You Support or Oppose Donald Trump's Decision to Withdraw from the

Likewise, Trump has moved relatively quickly on his promises concerning trade issues and other treaties, which under US law offer a number of opportunities for unilateral executive decisions. Within a few days of his inauguration, Trump signed an order to withdraw the United States from the Trans-Pacific Partnership (TPP)[34]. Trump dealt with the North American Free Trade Agreement (NAFTA) in a similar way, instructing officials within days of his inauguration to start renegotiating the trade deal, under the threat that he would terminate it. Although it is unclear if the president has the power to pull out of NAFTA without Congressional approval, these negotiations are ongoing.

Some of Trump's other promises related to trade relations haven't been fulfilled as of yet, such as his promise to label China a currency manipulator and block its entrance into the World Trade Organization. But, moving into his second year in office, perhaps his biggest trade issues have been his aluminum and steel tariffs. He used a provision in US law that allows him to impose tariffs in "national security" situations, despite the lack of any evidence that such is the case. Trade analysts say that his moves, which target allies in Europe and North America, show an increasing hostility toward international trade agreements and disregard for the rule of law. Trump apparently believes that trade wars and threats are good negotiating techniques, and that they may get economic concessions favouring the United States[35].

Finally, we should mention that Trump has been able to implement various restrictions on immigration. Some of the most

---

Main International Agreement That Tries to Address Climate Change? Do You Feel That Way Strongly or Somewhat?", *Washingtonpost.com*, 7 June 2017.

[34] However, in a move that appeared to surprise his own team, in April 2018, Trump instructed his administration officials to look into rejoining the TPP or modifying the agreement. Not surprisingly, the 11 countries already part of the agreement reacted cautiously, saying they were glad the United States was interested in trade, but that it was probably too late to renegotiate the deal.

[35] H. Long and S. Mufson, "Trump Thinks He's Saving Trade. The Rest of the World Thinks He's Blowing It Up", *Washington Post*, 2 June 2018.

prominent are a travel ban on visitors from several predominantly Muslim countries in Africa and the Middle East, which are prevented from receiving visas unless they can prove a relationship with someone in the US; and efforts to crack down on illegal immigration, especially from Latin American countries along the US-Mexico border, through stepped-up policing and harsher treatment of detainees. Trump has had to modify some of these in response to legal challenges and the protests of his own party members, but most of them are currently in effect.

In contrast, Trump has struggled to implement positive reforms that require Congressional approval. To mention a prominent example, Trump's promise to fully fund the construction of a 2000-mile border wall to be reimbursed by the country of Mexico is either a "promise broken" or "in-the-works," depending on the perspective. The key problem is that the effort required an estimated US$25 billion, which had to be authorised by Congress. Congress only authorised US$1.6 billion in the spring of 2018, and specified that this money could only be used for some new fencing and maintenance on existing fencing and walls along about 100 miles of the border. None of the money could be used for any of the "border wall" prototypes that Trump visited and promoted in his speeches. As for making Mexico pay for this wall, the Washington Post cited a telephone call transcript between Trump and Enrique Peña Nieto where Trump said he wasn't going to press Mexico on this, but that he couldn't say anything because it would damage him politically [36].

We see a similar pattern in other policy promises involving new laws and appropriations. The clearest example is the effort to repeal the Affordable Care Act, or Obamacare, and replace it with health savings accounts which requires congressional approval. In 2017 Congress was unable to pass a new health care bill or repeal the existing one because a number of Republicans

---

[36] M. Kelly, "Fact-Checking President Trump's Claims on Immigration", *Washingtonpost.com*, 7 May 2018.

refused to support the measure. Instead, Trump and Republican members of Congress subsequently worked to undermine the ACA in a piecemeal fashion. For example, the 2018 tax reform bill (the only major domestic reform passed under Trump as of this writing) repealed the penalty on the individual mandate, a key provision that required people who could afford health care to purchase health insurance.

Thus, Trump has had limited, if real success at implementing his policy agenda. Most of these successes affect US allies, undermining support for the US and threatening the global liberal order; these are significant concerns. At home, however, Trump has been able to accomplish much less, and Congress remains astonishingly gridlocked. Congress passed a major tax reform in 2018 and a spending bill that boosted defense spending, but progress on other signature issues such as immigration and health care reform has been stymied, and looming challenges such as Social Security (pension) reform and the fiscal deficit have been almost entirely ignored. Obviously, this mixed outcome reflects the unique context of the US, where overall support for Trump's brand of nationalist populism remains in the minority. Unlike nationalist populists in other countries, including some considered in this volume, Trump and his allies simply do not control enough pieces of the American political system to swiftly and easily enact preferred legislation, even with formal control of both houses of Congress.

The Impact on Liberal Democracy and Political Pluralism

Scholars who study populism note that populism can be beneficial for some aspects of democratic representation by helping incorporate forgotten segments of the electorate. This happens by increasing their political participation, dignifying their viewpoints, and including their concerns on the political agenda[37].

---

[37] C. Mudde and C. Rovira Kaltwasser (eds.), *Populism in Europe and the Americas:*

But once in power, populists tend to have a negative impact on core institutions of democratic competition, such as civil liberties, the fairness of elections, and the separation of powers[38]. Populists in office also tend to ignore the policy concerns and dignity of their opponents, thus undermining their opponents' democratic representation[39]. Importantly, these effects seem to be largely independent of whether populists are nationalist or another ideological stripe; populists of the left are just as strongly associated with these negative impacts. What matters most is the strength of the leader's populist rhetoric.

Thus far, Trump's presidency has presented only modest challenges to the institutions of liberal democracy, and political pluralism remains intact. Although Trump's questionable interaction with Russians during the 2016 campaign is garnering headlines, and this investigation is still playing out, there have been no real attempts to tamper with election quality. Onerous voter registration laws and gerrymandering in individual states are ongoing concerns (election administration is controlled by state and local governments under the US Constitution), but these predate the Trump presidency, and Trump has not publicly attempted to defend these questionable practices. Certainly there has been no effort at constitutional rewriting (at least, not yet). But there are worrying signs that liberal democracy is being challenged in other areas, with the implication that more could follow.

The clearest challenge is to civil liberties, especially attacks on press freedom and freedom of expression. The largest category of tweets since Trump became president is about "fake

Threat or Corrective to Democracy?, Cambridge, Cambridge University Press, 2012.
[38] R.A. Huber and C.H. Schimpf, "Friend or Foe? Testing the Influence of Populism on Democratic Quality in Latin America", *Political Studies*, vol. 64, no. 4, 2016a, pp. 872-89; S. Levitsky and J. Loxton, "Populism and Competitive Authoritarianism in the Andes", *Democratization*, vol. 20, no. 1, 2013, pp. 107-36.
[39] S.P. Ruth and K.A. Hawkins, "Populism and Democratic Representation in Latin America", in R.C. Heinisch, C. Holtz-Bacha, and O. Mazzoleni (eds.), *Political Populism: A Handbook*, Baden-Baden, Nomos, 2017, pp. 255-74.

news," his famous catch-phrase to criticise media coverage he doesn't personally like or that doesn't flatter him. In a search of his tweets since 2017, more than 230 had this phrase, as in the following from May 2018:

> The Fake Mainstream Media has, from the time I announced I was running for President, run the most highly sophisticated & dishonest Disinformation Campaign in the history of politics. No matter how well WE do, they find fault. But the forgotten men & women WON, I'm President!

These "fake news" tweets don't include all of his personal attacks on members of the press, which number in the hundreds, and by some counts have reached 1,000 or more. While by themselves these tweets are harmless, they contribute to an environment in which portions of the electorate turn to highly questionable, politicised media sources and have encouraged threats and attacks against individual journalists and media outlets.

Responding to these threats, major international press freedom organisations conducted a mission to the United States in early 2018 to collect data on the increasing problems. Their report details a growing number of challenges facing media workers, including prosecutions of whistleblowers, restrictions on public information, and physical attacks and arrests of journalists. They note that although media organisations have been criticised in the past, the most prominent intimidation of journalists now comes from the President and his aides. The report's authors say that these attacks on the press have created an environment where people "feel emboldened to denigrate reporters personally" and that "threats are considered a routine part of journalists' everyday lives"[40]. Not surprisingly, Freedom House's Freedom of the Press report for 2017 shows a downward shift

---

[40] Article 19, Committee to Protect Journalists, Index on Censorship, International Press Institute, and Reporters without Borders, "Press Freedom under Threat: International Press Freedom Mission to the United States", London, 2018, pp. 28-29.

of two points for the United States on the political environment[41]. And the 2018 World Press Freedom Index dropped the United States two places in the rankings mostly based on the media environment created by Trump[42]. A possible positive outcome from the increased hostility is that a number of media organisations are assessing their work to make sure it is held to a high standard for accuracy, and a number of organisations are taking a renewed interest in promoting basic rights, such as freedom of expression and press freedom.

Another area in which the Trump administration is challenging liberal democracy is the separation of powers. Specifically, Trump is questioning norms concerning executive privilege and the president's relationship to independent agencies associated with the judiciary, such as the Attorney General and the Department of Justice. The Department of Justice is currently overseeing a special investigation into the alleged involvement of the Russian government in the Trump campaign. Trump bitterly resents the investigation and has repeatedly attacked those managing it, including at times his handpicked Attorney General, who recused himself from directly overseeing the investigation because a conflict of interest. So far these attacks have been mostly verbal, and Trump has restrained himself from firing the special counsel in charge of the investigation – but he has intimated several times that he would like to. He did fire the FBI director and some of his assistants, allegedly because of their involvement in the investigation[43]. Trump has fired many other cabinet officials as well[44], something within his prerogative as president, but he is famous for announcing his firings through highly public tweets before any official letter

[41] Freedom House, "Freedom of the Press 2017: United States", 2017.
[42] Reporters without Borders, "United States: Trump Exacerbates Press Freedom's Steady Decline", RSF, 2018.
[43] M.D. Shear and M. Apuzzo, "F.B.I. Director James Comey Is Fired by Trump", *The New York Times*, 20 January 2018.
[44] C. Graham, "'You're Fired!': Who Donald Trump Has Sacked and Who Has Resigned during His Time as President", *The Telegraph*, 1 August 2017.

is sent. He insists on a high level of personal loyalty, and he seems to run the executive branch unconstrained by professional norms of conduct.

The encroachment on the separation of powers can also be seen in Trump's use of executive orders. Although intended as a device to execute the law, US presidents sometimes use these to legislate, because executive orders can effectively only be overturned by a 2/3 vote of Congress or (what is more common) through judicial review. Thus, they encroach on the separation of powers. Although the use of questionable executive orders has increased in recent years as presidents attempted to circumvent gridlocked legislatures, Trump has used them at roughly twice the pace of Presidents Obama or Bush[45].

Again, many of these challenges pale in comparison to those experienced in other countries where populists have come to power with higher levels of support and a more radical platform. Trump has not attempted to jail journalists and promote legal censorship, he has not fired judges and stacked the courts, nor has he sought control of electoral agencies (difficult to manage, given state control over elections). Indeed, he has largely avoided any electoral hijinks on behalf of Republican candidates. Most of his support for Republicans has come in the form of endorsements and public appearances – often without any visible benefit for the candidate. At the time of this writing, Republican candidates have lost most of the by-elections for Congress and state offices, a source of consternation for party leaders. The odds are high that Democrats will make significant gains in Congress and in state offices in the 2018 midterms.

Trump has also avoided any effort to rewrite the Constitution. This would be an unusual step in the US, where conservatives revere the document as divinely inspired and have long argued for legal interpretations of its text using the principle of original intent. No previous populist movement in the US has argued

---

[45] The American Presidency Project, "Executive Orders: Washington-Trump", The United Nations, 2018; "United Nations Treaty Collection", Treaties.un.org. 2018.

for doing away with the Constitution. That said, constitutional conventions and amendments are mainstays of contemporary populist movements in other countries, where they provide not only a moment for symbolically reasserting the people's control over democracy, but a tool for strengthening and consolidating control over the government. If Trump remains in office for a second term, and especially if he struggles against a reluctant Congress or independent agencies, it would not be surprising to see his supporters pursue constitutional amendments that could, for example, eliminate term limits.

Conclusions

Nationalist populism under Trump has defied some initial expectations. Trump continues to claim to defend working Americans against a corrupt establishment, and he promotes a set of policies geared towards trade protectionism, the defense of traditional culture, and the exclusion of so-called undesirable or dangerous immigrants. He has not moderated this message in any effort to broaden his coalition, but has increasingly played to a relatively narrow and faithful Republican base. The result is a continuation of earlier trends towards affective polarisation and partisan sorting in the electorate, and a very mixed record of incomplete policy successes and failures. Trump's impact on democracy has not been as severe as his worst critics feared, but it has not been positive either, with attacks on the media and the assertion of executive powers.

We have argued that the modest impact of nationalist populism reflects some unique conditions in the US, conditions that set it apart from populism in regions such as Central and Eastern Europe, where populists attract much stronger electoral support and have had more serious consequences for policy and democratic institutions. However, Trump has only been in office for a little over 18 months, and we may wonder what the future holds. In other countries with populist leaders, the more significant effects of populism are not felt until the leaders have been in government for several years, with time to cement their following while chiseling away at institutions.

Prediction in the US is difficult, however. One reason is that the impact of populism depends not just on the strength of the government's populist and nationalist discourses, but also on the personality of the leader. Trump has unusual confidence in his own skill and judgment and demands the loyalty of his advisors and cabinet officials; he frequently switches positions depending on what he hears from a select number of media sources; and he is very concerned about his public image. This makes legislative policy success more difficult, but it also jeopardises the informal norms that govern so much of US politics at the federal level.

Another reason is that much depends on the opposition and its ability to field moderate candidates in a two-party system. Trump and the Republican's current weakness place the Democratic Party in a stronger position to retake control of the government. But populism tends to polarise, and this could lead strong partisans within the party to push for more radical candidates that would make centrist voters turn to Trump and his Republican supporters. Recent primary elections suggest that this is not happening, however; moderate candidates among the Democrats have proven very successful at defeating radical challengers, and incumbents are responding to their base. In many ways, Trump's national populism reflects underlying problems and challenges of US politics today.

3. Populism and Nationalism in CEE: Two of a Perfect Pair?

Radoslaw Markowski

Today, the notion of nationalism falls behind that of populism in popularity, references, and usage, yet a simple glance at a longer historical time frame shows how attractive the former term used to be in the history of human thought and the social sciences. The relationship between the two is complex, if only because of its many flavours and manifestations in reality, and the definitions and models offered in the academic discourse. At this point, several caveats seem necessary.

First, the Central and Eastern Europe (CEE) region is by comparative standards fairly diverse – ethnically, historically, religiously (presence of three Christian denominations plus Islam), as well as in terms of the very existence of statehood and nation-states in the region. For this reason, and in order to avoid too much intricacy, the countries of former Yugoslavia, the Baltic states, and Romania will not be covered. Our analysis will focus mainly on Poland and Hungary with a few glimpses from Bulgaria, Slovakia, and the Czech Republic.

Second, both nationalism and populism are temporally fluid cncepts: they have histories of their own depending on the particular historical legacies of a given nation-state.

Third, the notion of populism is vague and contaminated with many a- (or anti-) democratic and a- (or anti-)liberal phenomena. In our everyday parlance, almost anything that challenges the liberal democracy can be called populism. As a result of its alleged unlimited travelling capacity across world's political cultures, the "populist basket" is filled with far too many and problematic phenomena. Thus, we first need a clear definition of the term.

Populism

Among the many possible definitions, in this chapter, populism will be defined as an ideology that "considers society to be ultimately separated into two homogeneous and antagonistic groups, 'the pure people' versus 'the corrupt elite', and which argues that politics should be an expression of the *volonté générale* (general will) of the people"[1].

However, additional specifications are needed. First, populism is considered to be a peculiar type of ideology – a *thin-centrered ideology*. Unlike *thick* ideologies, it allegedly lacks a coherent political programme. It often goes together with these ideologies proper ("thicker"), and as a consequence is characterised as "chameleonic". Second, populism rejects institutional mediation, discards pluralism and tolerance. Third, it often assumes internal homogeneity of The People against the heterogeneity of the "aliens". Fourth, populism typically occurs in crisis and is related quite often to the rejection of modernity. For this reasons, many consider it to be an episodic phenomenon that vanishes with the successful termination of the crisis. Fifth, in many instances, experts on populism assume a charismatic leader is a necessary condition for populism to occur.

In my view, in order to understand the essence of populism, the one that pops up in the CEE region in particular, one should try to name its "negative" – the opposite phenomena that populism is either in "ontological conflict" with, or the ones it rejects. For the latter case, two such phenomena are pluralism and tolerance. My argument is that we need to add another

---

[1] C. Mudde, "The Populist Zeitgeist", *Government and Opposition*, vol. 39, no. 4, 2004, pp. 541-563, cit. p. 543.

one: meritocracy. Populism denies the complexity of the world, rejects most economic and social theories, refutes scientific achievements, expertise, causal relationships, "means-tested" policy decision-making, etc. It upholds crude "simplicism". In my view, the current dire political developments in the CEE countries are to a large extent better explained by the concept of "simplicism" than populism. In the last part of the chapter I will devote more space to describe this issue as well as present some preliminary analysis for Poland.

One should also critically revisit the assumption that populism surfaces typically during crises. It frequently certainly does so, but recent ominous developments (in Poland and Slovakia, in particular) under absolutely favourable socio-economic conditions attest to the contrary.

Finally, the main problem with describing, explaining, and assessing populist parties is that their "life expectancy" is low; most of them either disappear after one or two electoral cycles or remain irrelevant sofa parties. Of course, Fidesz in Hungary and PiS in Poland are examples to the contrary, yet my main point is that these are not "populist proper" parties, even if they display strong populist components during electoral campaigns. Equally often, the populist phenomenon is combined with nationalism, religious fundamentalism, Euroscepticism, or anti-cosmopolitanism, and unjust macro-economic conditions and/or failures in redistributive fairness.

Nationalism

Nationalism belongs to those ideologies which Mudde would certainly classify as "thick" ones. In this chapter, with "thick" ideology (e.g. nationalism) I refer to a relatively coherent and comprehensive set of ideas, which explains and evaluates the existing social predicament, helps people grasp their "place" and role in society, and offers them a programme and a plan of action aimed at changing the – allegedly grim – reality. It is a certain type of cognitive map of reality, a sketch of the future ideal society, and a plan of action to achieve it[2].

Nationalism essentially holds that the nation and the nation-state are fundamental values, which are aimed at mobilising the political will of the people for the defense against aliens. This is its core. Additional elements have to be included in order to allow for a more adequate description of CEE countries[3]. First, for those countries that have been imperial powers (Prussia/Germany, France etc.) the logic of nation-state played a unifying and expansive role. In CEE, nationalism has played a defensive and liberating role and has been delayed compared to Western Europe by a century or so. Second, nationalism has a cultural component, a complex bundle of language, historical symbols, literature, and myths about the nation's genesis and legacy; the less a given country was able to achieve a recognised international status and unquestioned borders with its "people", the more the historical narrative resembles megalomaniac, "crafted" past legacies and historical "facts". Third, preoccupation with boundaries and their social consequences – who are "the people", and the universal versus exclusivist vision of ethnic groups living within the state's territory – poses a much more urgent problem in CEE than in the Western part of Europe[4].

Needless to stress that almost all countries of the CEE region were not existing as independent states in the XIX century when most Western European countries were emerging as strong nation-states. Delayed modernisation (save for Bohemia) and a short-lived interwar turbulent period of establishing their new borders; dramatic overpopulation of the rural areas, inhabited by significant groups of people hardly identifying with the

---

[2] J. Gerring, "Ideology: A definitional analysis", *Political Research Quarterly*, vol. 50, no. 4, 1997, pp. 957-994.

[3] E. Gellner, *Nations and Nationalism*, Oxford, Basil Blackwell, 1983; P. Alter, *Nationalism*, London, Edward Arnold, 1991; J. Breuilly (ed.), The Oxford handbook of the history of nationalism, Oxford, Oxford UP, 2013.

[4] E.J. Hobsbawm, *Nations and Nationalism Since 1780: Programme, Myth, Reality*, Cambridge, Cambridge University Press, 1992; G. Germani, *Authoritarianism, fascism, and national populism*, New Brunswick, NJ, Transaction Books, 1978.

new state; the extraordinarily dire consequences of the Great Depression, resulting in a political switch towards authoritarianism or outright fascism (again, save for Czechoslovakia); all this paints a good picture of the situation in the CEE region in the first half of the XX century. Then came the hecatomb of WWII, which in some countries (Poland in particular) contributed to dramatic changes in ethnic composition, a major modification of the social structures, and the erosion of key cultural mega-values, not to mention the consequences of the installment of communism, with its dramatic change in property rights, mode of production, and political and civil rights[5].

Central Eastern European Overview

The new millennium witnessed an upsurge in the popularity of populist, xenophobic, radical (mainly right-wing, but occasionally also left-wing) parties. They range from Vlaams Belang (formerly Vlaams Block), Lega (until recently Lega Nord), Wilder's PVV (Party for Freedom), the Dansk Folkerparti and – while a bit different – the French Front National, the Austrian FPÖ (Freedom Party of Austria) and many more. They differ. First of all, the older radical/populist parties (Front National, Vlaams Blok, Lega Nord and FPÖ) were engrained in the past European xenophobic/nationalist politics. More recent parties, found today in the same (broad) populist basket, comprising the True Finns, the Dutch PVV, the Swedish Democrats, the Danish Peoples Party and the like, are more liberal-democratic and less radical. By and large these newer parties are also distancing themselves from primitive biological racism or border-driven identities and nationalism, partly because they themselves are often offspring of former mainstream liberal parties. Their leaders, representatives, and followers truly believe they are the "solution" to the current dire problems of liberal

---

[5] P. Latawski (ed.), *Contemporary Nationalism in East Central Europe*, London, MacmillanPress, 1995.

democracies, and a sort of effective correction to democratic failures, especially the quality of representation.

The variation of the CEE political landscape is by no means less complex. Starting from similarities, parties that evidently resemble the old Western European xenophobic ones in the CEE region are: the Bulgarian Ataka, the Hungarian Jobbik (certainly until the 2018 campaign), the Slovak SNS (Slovak National Party), and the PRM (Greater Romania Party). Their programme is distinctly xenophobic, at times bordering what Mudde calls "nativism"[6]. The region was also populated by other non-liberal democratic phenomena, such as the LPR (League of Polish Families) or Self-defence (Samoobrona), which rapidly emerged and equally swiftly disappeared[7], the Hungarian MIEP (Justice and Life Party) and the Czech Republicans.

Populism and Nationalism in the CEE

Many commentators, researchers, and thinkers mix up populism with nationalism or frequently misperceive their relationship. The problem is even more acute in the CEE region, characterised by a shorter state history, complicated nation-building problems – including questionable boundaries – and disputed historical legacies. To quote the famous Linz/Stepan motto "no state, no democracy", for both populists and nationalists, the important question is who (legally and symbolically) belongs to the nation and comprises "the people"[8].

I submit that, to understand the current illiberal and non-democratic turn in CEE countries, the widely accepted Mudde's definition of populism is most of the time (though depending on the country) inadequate. This is not to say that the

---

[6] C. Mudde, *The relationship between immigration and nativism in Europe and North America*, Washington, DC, Migration Policy Institute, 2012.

[7] See R. Markowski and J. Tucker, "Euroskepticism and the Emergence of Political Parties in Poland", *Party Politics*, vol. 16, no. 4, 2010, pp. 523-548.

[8] J.J. Linz and A. Stepan, *Problems of Democratic Transition and Consolidation. Southern Europe, South America, and Post-Communist Europe*, Baltimore, The Johns Hopkins University Press, 1996.

concept as offered by Mudde will not find empirical evidence in the CEE region. Quite to the contrary, the existence of such a phenomenon can fairly easily be documented; yet, the results will hardly be – to use statistical jargon – of impressive explained variance. For one, most of the CEE countries had started their journey from an authoritarian regime towards democracy under the assumption that, under the new regime, all of "the people" would have a say in politics and societal life, unlike under the previous one. Secondly, in some countries, most notably Poland, in the late 1970s and 1980s, the main conflict has been dubbed "Us vs Them"; "them" being the party *apparatchiks* and *nomenklatura*. To be sure, in historical time, two decades are a somewhat short period to create "frozen" cleavages, hierarchical divides and the like, legitimising the "elite vs mass" narrative. In the region, most of those who have become the "elite" in the early 1990s were hardly heirs of aristocratic families, successors of capitalist entrepreneurial fortunes, or land estates owners' families; not even upper middle-class transgenerational status transmission played a role (with the possible exception of the Czech Republic). The new elites were a complex mixture of the old intelligentsia, university graduates, vibrant grassroot economic entrepreneurs, and some post-communist "*entrepreneurchiks*" (the offspring of the former "*apparatchiks*"). Right from the beginning, however, CEE populism was heavily loaded with patriotic narratives, nationalist sentiments, historical nostalgia, and sheer xenophobia. In some instances, this strong nationalist element was understandable, as completely new nation-states appeared on the European map. This chaotic phase lasted at least until the end of the second millennium. On the other hand, the first nationalist/radical/populist instances in the CEE region occurred in the early 1990s: Sladek's Republicans in the Czech Republic, Csurka's MIEP, HZDS (People's Party - Movement for a Democratic Slovakia) and SNS in Slovakia, and KPN (Confederation of Independent Poland). By the new millennium, however, most of them had ceased to exist: their attack on the alleged elite did not work, partly because it was hard to claim there was an "elite proper". All of them, however, had a strong nationalist edge, with ethnic aversion towards neighbouring country-nations being the core element.

The second generation of parties belonging to this political family occurred around or after the entry to the EU, mobilising support typically by referring to the purported challenges and threat resulting from the EU entry. In most instances – this was certainly the case with the Polish Samoobrona (Self-Defence), LPR, the Hungarian Jobbik, the Bulgarian Ataka, the Slovak Smer, to name just the most important ones: all of them (to a different degree) have been using a mixture of populist and nationalist appeals. To be sure, were we to look at the region's "political and party supply" via four-fold taxonomy lenses (created by juxtaposing populist and nationalist dimensions), all of them would unveil a clear dominance of the nationalist element over the populist one. In other words, among the anti-systemic, radical parties (uncritically labeled "populist"), one finds that most of them share a distinct appeal to the "nation" and a pretty horizontal view of politics while few of them (those whose dominant element is addressed to the "people" *en masse*) are accompanied by a vertical conflicting cleavage. The Bulgarian Ataka, the Polish LPR, the Hungarian Jobbik, and earlier in the 1990s the Polish KPN, the Hungarian MIEP and the Slovak SNS are cases in point. A caveat, however, is due here: CEE nationalism (at times closer to patriotism, at times to racial xenophobia) has moderate linkage to what has been the main concern of Western European "populist, far-right" parties like Vlaams Belang, the PVV in the Netherlands, the Danish Peoples Party, which focused mainly on globalisation issues, the threat of Islam and – in a way – a neoliberal approach to economy, redistribution, and civic concerns. Shortly: Western counterparts are not prone to territorial nationalism and/or biological racism, which can evidently be traced in Jobbik's, Ataka's or SNS's programmes and public appearances of their leaders.

Central Eastern European Case Studies

Bulgaria

Before discussing the Hungarian and Polish cases in more detail, let me start with another interesting one: Bulgaria. There are several reasons for this: first, Bulgaria has had a decade of populist-free politics of a classical left-right or post-communist vs democratic divide with a specific role – sometimes a "king-maker" – i.e., the ethnic minority (Turkish) party called Movement for Rights and Freedom (MRF). Until the end of the 1990s, the party system looked stable, voter volatility had been relatively low, and no charismatic leadership was present. Instead, there was a rather classic party organisation structure. Second, the first populist wave (of a very specific kind) occurred when at the end of the 1990s deep crisis haunting Bulgaria, the former tsar Simeon II took the quite unexpected decision to return to Bulgaria and contest elections. The short electoral campaign of this new entity (its official existence prior to the election was less than 3 months) called National Movement Simeon II (NMSII) won 42% of the popular vote and precisely half of the parliamentary seats[9].

Classifying this political movement, though, is problematic, mainly because there is a clear distinction between what occurred during the electoral campaign and the discontinuity in its governmental performance and policies. In favour of a populist label speak the following facts: (a) Simeon II's campaign was anything but programmatic, it promised fulfillment of most of the expectations Bulgarians had at the time; (b) his address was to "the people" as a whole without references to any division within society, (c) except for suggestions that the former political elite was corrupted; (d) in opposition to this elite,

---

[9] For details, see D. Smilov, "Bulgaria", in G. Mesežnikov, O. Gyárfášová and D. Smilov (eds.), *Populist Politics and Liberal Democracy in Central and Eastern Europe*, 2008.

his personal integrity was part of his charismatic appeal; (e) no ideological foundations of the Movement had been offered to the public, quite the reverse – his position was that, in the new millennium, XX century ideologies are irrelevant.

At the same time, his enormous popularity that translated into a vibrant political mobilisation resulted directly from his extraordinary status of former tsar. He behaved differently from the Bulgarian political class, spoke slowly and quietly, in an very uncommon way, with dignity, using words and expressions long forgotten in the Bulgarian public debate, and even had a bit of a strange accent. In sum, one can hardly imagine more of an elitist candidate than His Majesty. Moreover, his appeal was more to the Bulgarian nation than to "the people" as defined by liberal tradition. Finally, during the campaign he did make contradictory policy promises, like achieving budgetary balance and stability simultaneously with welfare generosity and substantive tax cuts. For such miracles to be accomplished, he employed Western economic and financial experts, which in the first year of his government introduced policies that can hardly be called populist, rather the reverse: many were lucid liberal economic recipes for the relatively backward and malfunctioning economy. Very soon, support for the movement declined significantly, and the movement registered as a party, soon to join the European liberal party family.

The second phase of populist nationalism occurred in the 2005 election when a non-political person, a former journalist, organised a party named Ataka, which entered the parliament and became the main opposition party. The peculiar character of Ataka was its undeniable xenophobic and nationalistic feature, relying on very aggressive language (racist against Roma in particular), public narratives coming as close as can be to a hate speech pattern, loaded with numerous conspiracy theories, and a strong penchant for emotions, with little indication of practical solutions. National integrity and national interest were the dominant language of the party to the extent it insisted on banning the "Turkish" MRF party on ethnic grounds. Its appeal was to the

Bulgarian people, not any other people that might – accidentally in their view – dwell on the Bulgarian land. The party presented also an anti-elitist edge, yet its core political profile is nationalist/ xenophobic and only complementarily a populist one.

Experts of the Bulgarian political arena also treat Boiko Borisov's GERB (Citizens for European Development of Bulgaria) party as a manifestation of populism. In this instance it is even more problematic, even if certain features of populist repertoire are in use by the party and Borisov himself. First, indeed, he is close to what we could call a charismatic leader, someone from the grassroots, who speaks common people's language (not to say jargon), a personality of the media much more than of mainstream politics. GERB has no clear ideological or even programmatic stance, even if it belongs to the People's party bloc in the EU parliament. GERB is sceptical about the necessity of institutional intermediation between "the people" and the government; it seems to them that a talented popular leader and broad media coverage can substitute for the traditional channels of political communication. The problem with GERB and his leader is that it also fits very well the description of a regular catch-all party, since the economic policies of the GERB government are rather predictable and constrained by the global and EU rules.

Hungary

The Hungarian party system has been considered for a long time to be the only institutionalised and predictable party system in the CEE region. Already by the late 1990s, it was divided in two blocs: the left-liberal and the conservative/nationalist, with very low, single-digit voter volatility, clear polarisation of both political elites and society, and virtually no annoying newcomers to the system, at least until ten/fifteen years ago. Its simple institutional political infrastructure (a single chamber parliament, an indirectly elected and weak president, the whole executive power in the hands of the prime minister) has little veto points.

In the case of Hungary, the radical parties started to emerge right from the beginning of the transformation even if, at first, they remained marginal. The first was the MIEP, led by Istvan Csurka, a party in favour of ethnically pure "people", with a clear anti-Semitic edge, frequently broadened to show disrespect or even hatred towards all "aliens" (non-Magyars), but also against globalism and foreign interests – allegedly dominant in Hungary. In procedural terms, it was a classical "law and order" programmatic appeal. Only once, in 1998, the MIEP made it to the parliament; the period after 2002 was characterised by a slow but steady decline. In more or less the same timeframe a new party, Jobbik, gained prominence and – in a way – programmatically substituted the MIEP. Jobbik is equally "concerned" with minorities, Roma in particular, but also very much with the fate of Hungarians abroad. In terms of foreign policy it openly claims post-Trianon suffering to be the most important experience for Hungarians. Electorally, the party turned out to be much more successful than the MIEP, attracting up to 1/5 of the active adult population. Born in the period when Fidesz had been in opposition, the party had promised general, radical change of Hungarian politics once in power. It is hard to estimate to what extent Jobbik is a byproduct of Orban's vision of the new socio-political order as well as his willingness to have a radical right-wing party, placing – allegedly –Fidesz more to the centre of the political spectrum.

Both parties are anti-liberal, anti-global, and present disrespect for the institutional order of the country pointing to their populist character, yet their nationalist ingredient seems to be more evident and in fact, dominant.

The status, deeds, and policies of Fidesz will be discussed after describing the Polish case, in comparative perspective to the Polish PiS (Law and Justice).

Poland

It should be emphasised that even in the same country there is room for more than one party of nationalist-populist lineage. The Poland of the early new millennium might serve as an interesting case. One of the two parties – Samoobrona – first achieved political representation in the 2005 election as a direct heir of a radical peasant trade union, famous for its violent public behaviour already in the 1990s. As a party, it presented a clear example of reckless economic policy ideas, rejecting the then-elites and institutional mediation between the government and the masses, as well as opposing EU membership on purely economic grounds. Briefly: Samoobrona openly discarded the particular deal Poland made with the EU and its economic consequences, yet claiming to be in favour of EU membership had there been a better arrangement with the EU. Thus, it presented clear populist elements along with nationalist ones, belonging to "economic" nationalism. In addition, Samoobrona displayed a rather neutral attitude towards the religious domain, and no direct links to the Catholic Church, which is an important feature in Polish politics.

The other party, the League of Polish Families, displayed a different political profile – an ethnic-driven nationalism coupled with religious fundamentalism. The LPR was not Eurosceptic in the pragmatic sense Samoobrona was: it was entirely anti-European, siding against Enlightenment values, rationality, civic culture, ethnic tolerance, and so on. Shortly: it rejected the very idea of joining or even closely cooperating with Europe on ideological and axiological grounds. Europe, with its liberal values, has been considered a threat to Polishness and its main component, namely Catholicism. The followers of this party were of low educational attainment, rather poor, devout believers from the countryside, twice more likely female. The economic, redistributive element was visible in their political appeal, yet it was clearly a corollary of the alleged socio-cultural injustice. Detailed differences between the two, their genesis and their followers can be found elsewhere[10]. However, both parties disappeared from the Polish political arena only three years into its EU membership, after the EU funds reached the Polish countryside. This is not to say that their Eurosceptic voters have disappeared, yet PiS was able to attract only a small portion of their followers.

The next wave of parties contesting elections on nationalist and populist grounds was first visible in the 2015 elections, both presidential and parliamentary. First, a grassroot out-of-politics candidate (a rock singer) and a movement named after him – Kukiz'15 – attracted almost one in ten of the active Polish electorate. Its appeal resembles that of "Samoobrona" in its definite focus on economic and redistributive issues. The movement unveils also a clear anti-institutional edge, disbelief in parliamentarism, representative democracy, and advocates direct democracy instead. Thus, Kukiz'15's brand of nationalism-populism is more of an economic nature and clearly anti-institutional, yet it is hard to claim it appeals to "the people" in general: the addressee of its appeal are rather those who lost out in the economic transition.

Let's now turn to the main candidate for the nationalist-populist label: the ruling PiS party. As in the case of the Hungarian Fidesz, I will discuss PiS's peculiarities in a comparative manner, but before going for the comparison, a few introductory remarks. PiS (and its direct predecessor PC) has been in the Polish party arena since its democratic transition almost thirty years ago. Its prominent leaders, the twin brothers Kaczynski, have been involved in Polish politics ever since. As a consequence, one of the stipulations for populist parties – that their leadership emerges from outside the political elite – is, in PiS's case, not met. In the 1990s, the PC (and from 2001 onwards, PiS) clearly belonged to the conservative family, and its support has fluctuated between 5 and 10%. The programmatic shift occurred for the first time around the referendum and entry to

---

[10] R. Markowski and J. Tucker (2010).

the EU, indicating a definite embrace of more nationalist and Eurosceptic narratives, and for a second time, after the 2010 airplane crash in which the then-President Lech Kaczynski lost his life, contributing to further radicalisation, divisiveness, and "zero-sum-game" approach to politics[11].

Hungarian-Polish comparison

In comparing the Polish and Hungarian cases, I submit that, rather than concentrating on the alleged cleavage between corrupted elites and flawless "people", one has to look at the peculiarities of the illiberal and non-democratic new order being created in both countries. For Poland, I opt to call it either "authoritarian clientelism"[12] or "simplicism": the former resembles more an ideology, whereas the latter is what I consider one of the manifestations of a core element of populism (see next section). In Hungary, Orban's regime essence is even more obscure – it is simultaneously authoritarian, illiberal, xenophobic, populist, radical-right nationalist, but at the same time more sophisticated, deliberative, aideological or "multi-ideological" as I've tried to explain elsewhere[13]. *In view of recent developments an author like Magyar (2016) even defines it a "mafia state"*[14].

Let us at this point recall parts of Magyar's (2016; 2018)[15]

---

[11] See R. Markowski, "The Polish parliamentary election of 2015: a free and fair election that results in unfair political consequences", *West European Politics*, vol. 39, no. 6, 2016, pp. 1-12; M. Żerkowska-Balas, I. Lyubashenko, and A. Kwiatkowska, "Determinanty preferencji wyborczych: Polska w latach 1997-2015", *Studia Socjologiczne*, vol. 223, no. 4, 2016, pp. 69-96.

[12] R. Markowski, "Backsliding into Authoritarian Clientelism: The Case of Poland", in P. Guasti and Z. Mansfeldova (eds.), *Democracy under Stress: Changing Perspectives on Democracy, Governance and their Measurement*, Prague, Institute of Sociology, CAS, 2018.

[13] R. Markowski, "Wprowadzenie", in B. Magyar (ed.), *Węgry. Anatomia państwa mafijnego*, Warszawa, Magam, 2018. [(in Polish) "Introduction" in Hungary. Anatomy of a Mafia State]

[14] B. Magyar, *Post-Communist Mafia State: The Case of Hungary*, Budapest, CEU Press, 2016.

[15] B. Magyar, *Węgry. Anatomia państwa mafijnego...* cit.

proposal and critically discuss some of them. The author starts
with a claim that there are several fundamental similarities between the two regimes, among them: (a) the way they exert
power is not that of an ordinary government, but that of a "revolutionary" one; (b) as a consequence, they separate themselves
from the democratic transition of a quarter century ago (highly appreciated by the world elites) and interpret the history of
the peaceful, negotiated regime changes as a deal between elites
done behind the back of society, which is worth calling a "treason", using this to legitimise the necessity for the actual regime
change they implement; (c) by "nation" they refer to a community of people committed to an ideology, rather than a community of autonomous citizens, an argument that allows them
to exclude citizens critical of their policies and the regime, and
label them as representatives of alien interests; (d) they share a
particular form of Euroscepticism, and initiate what they deem
a "national liberation from Brussels'dictatorship" based on their
countries' classic "grievance politics" (not unlike the Soviet dictatorship in the post-WWII period), while continuing to expect
EU financial resources.

As Magyar claims there are, however, some key differences:
1) the Polish PiS regime is motivated by power and ideology. It
is a case of a ruling party that is centralised, led by party officials, in which the state is under bureaucratic control. While it
respects free-market competition and freedom of enterprise, the
party's favouritism and nepotism are visible. However, the loyal
elite is rewarded mainly with offices (not wealth), as it usually
happens in an "authoritarian" state. Magyar believes Poland is
far from the "point of no return" (to democracy) because – his
assessment goes – Poland has a proportional electoral system
and its divided executive power prevents excessive power concentration, thanks to a relatively strong presidential legitimacy.
It has strong traditions of social resistance. The configuration
of the Polish party system pushes PiS to the right edge, while
the centre is occupied by moderate right and liberal parties.
Poland enjoys free media, a strong presence of the opposition

in municipal governments, a strong centre beyond the capital, and autonomous free enterprise. 2) In contrast, the Hungarian regime uses power to achieve personal wealth, it is non-ideological or its ideology is applied cynically, its political decision making is not controlled by the legal, formalised organisations and is not socially controlled. As a consequence, the decisions are in the hands of an informal body of leadership, the "chef patron's court" (*polipburo*), and the ruling party is a sort of transmission belt where the patronal network is built on a centralised chain of command, revolving around patron-client relationships (*adopted political family*). It is a mafia state, where centralised and monopolised corruption exists to the benefit of the "adopted political family" wealth accumulation, if necessary, instruments of state coercion are employed (rent-seeking and corporate raiding). His view is that Hungary is dangerously to the point of no return to democracy, not least because of a peculiar political institutional infrastructure – disproportional and prone to manipulation electoral system, conducive to fraud, non-divided executive power, weak presidential legitimacy (indirectly elected President). All this is accompanied by the historical culture of "individuals' detached bargaining" with the regimes in power, the current central position of Fidesz in the party system (supplemented by the radical right-wing party, Jobbik), and a lack of either a moderate right-leaning party or a liberal one. Finally, the Hungarian case is depicted by Magyar as having contingent private enterprises, dependent on the patron-client links to the adopted political family. Local governments are at the mercy of both the central government and the regime. Media outlets are weak and there are very few remaining spaces for freedom of expression.

I do share many of the insightful Magyar's points, and I will only react to the ones I consider problematic. First, as to the alleged ideologically-driven motivation of the PiS leadership (Kaczynski personally) and a lack of such motivation on the part of the Fidesz leader. This was certainly true a decade ago (during the 2005-2007 PiS-led government), yet I am doubting whether it applies to the period after the 2015 Polish election. An ideological narrative – a mixture of nationalist megalomania and populist "generosity" – is present, of course, but the actions – widespread nepotism, fostering of clientelistic networks, non-meritocratic career advancements in the public sphere – attest to a definite dominance of a rational-cynical atmosphere aimed at creating a new "closed-access" social order. In his essay, Magyar assumes (somewhat implicitly) that an ideologically-driven illiberal politics is somehow "better" or more justified than the cynical treatment of different ideological threads used by Orban. I am not convinced; if we were to estimate the probability of a democratic revival in both countries, a scenario of dealing with a cynical, but somehow rational political leader, whose main concern is staying in power, seems easier than facing a stubborn, ideologically-oriented, intransigent leader, driven by a *fin de siècle* political mentality and understanding of the world, whose capacity to understand the new millennium is astonishingly limited[16].

The second major difference is the alleged Polish resistance and freedom-oriented traditions versus the Hungarian adaptive individualism and entrepreneurial-oriented spirit. One should be careful, first of all, in treating the numerous Polish revolts (1956, 1968, 1970, 1976, 1980-81, and 1987-89) as an indication of Polish longing for democracy, human rights, and civic freedoms. Only one single revolt, the 1968 students' one, was against suppression of individual freedoms, fought against censorship, and had little to do with economic shortages and material poverty. All other events were initiated by some form of protest against rising food prices, which eventually transformed into broader revolt against the regime. That was definitely the case of the 1980 protest, which had started as usual because of food shortages and then step by step moved the "Solidarity" from its pure trade union status to a social movement and ultimately in 1981 to a national-liberating political force aimed at getting

---

[16] For details see Markowski 2018c.

rid of Soviet dominance. "Self-restraining revolution", a term dubbed by J. Staniszkis, describes very well the developmental problem of revolts under Soviet control. Two mechanisms were at work, first – a determinism that forces a trade union to secure its basic rights to call for civil society's credentials, and since the latter were also unlikely to be achieved because of the external veto player (the Kremlin), it had to transform into a national liberation movement. At the same time, – remembering the Hungarian 1956 and Czechoslovak 1968 experiences with the Soviets – the movement had to cautiously act incrementally across these three phases. It did not work in Poland in 1980-81, while Brezhnev was in charge, but it did succeed a few years later under Gorbachev, himself willing to transform the Soviet Union into a "socialist country with a human face". As to the Hungarian case, I consider it pretty interesting in that – contrary to the Polish path – after the 1956 atrocities in Hungary, its communist leadership and most people decided there was no chance for a military exit from the Soviet-controlled communist camp. Instead, a well-designed and relatively successful (by "real socialism" standards) economic reform had been launched in the late 1960s and gave rise to an economy with some market mechanisms in the 1980s. Briefly, the Hungarian case is one of a rational, convergent effort to arrive at economic liberalisation first and, then, if the context allowed, democratise. In a way, the Kremlin was afraid of the wild revolts in Poland, but looked with interest and readiness for emulation at the Hungarian economic inventions. Moreover, the Hungarian leadership in the late 1980s, with Pozsgay, Nemeth, Nyers as the main movers towards exiting from communism, had a wise strategy and language of Marxism that pleased the ears of the Kremlin. Instead of talking about abandoning the Soviet allies, they preferred to speak of successful development of the "means of production" and "relations of production", thanks to their reformist strategy and the lagging behind of – unadjusted to their level – "superstructure". It was the Hungarian reformed communists who first announced in the late 1980s that some form of party pluralism was needed for the complex socialist society they had become. These facts should not be forgotten.

Third, the political science key dictum that "institutions matter" has proven correct on many counts. Yet, not always, in newly democratising countries, and the CEE in particular, the establishment of new democratic institutions has been – unlike in the majority of Western democracies – simultaneously accompanied by a full opening of the franchise to the whole adult population. Institutions, in such a new volatile environment, tend to be critically dependent on the readiness of the citizens, elites in particular, to adopt and play by the rules envisaged by them. Pearson emphasises this problem, by pointing that indeed formal institutional design matter, but equally do personalities who perform functions envisaged by these institutions[17]. It is worth underlining that Poland as a fist-comer to the transition in particular (but Hungary to a significantly higher extent than the rest of post-communist Europe) had a prolonged period of transition, with overlapping phases of exits from authoritarianism, incremental institution building, and consolidation. In Poland, from the initial Round Table talks to June 1989 election, from the so-called Small Constitution of 1992 to the final adoption of the latest Constitution in 1997, a learning process full of incidents and retrospectively changed and re-written rules as well as electoral law changes occurred. The result has been a creation of a culture of "rules negotiability" and "flexibility", a political mood of temporariness, and an increase in the pragmatic instrumentalisation of politics, which ultimately contributed to the low civic and public virtues of Poles[18]. Briefly, what at the time seemed to be a smooth, peaceful, and negotiated transition that allegedly is more conducive to full democratisation than violent *ruptura*, proved problematic. It seems that the visibility of a clear threshold that separates

---

[17] P. Pierson, *Politics in Time: History, Institutions, and Social Analysis*, Princeton, Princeton University Press, 2004.
[18] For details see R. Markowski, "Backsliding into Authoritarian Clientelism: The Case of Poland"…, cit.

the old regime from the new one was equally important for the democratic socialisation of the elites and citizens.

To summarise: in both countries, Poland and Hungary, a clearly illiberal and non-democratic trend is present. A backsliding into some sort of authoritarianism is evident, even though, as of 2018, to a different degree and with different consequences. In both countries, intransigent nationalism is on the rise, coupled with selective but widespread nepotism, corruption. It is harder to prove populism is dominant or even important. Of course, some elements are present, like disrespect for institutions, distinct violation of the rules of the political game, selective references to "the people" and the like. Yet, both Orban and Kaczynski have been in politics right from the beginning of the transformation, and prior to the period after 2010, they have been PMs of their respective countries. As a consequence, none of them can claim to be a new grassroot peoples' leader, given that both of them (and their parties) have played a role in post-1989 politics. Both have switched their ideological profile, from an ultra-liberal or mainstream conservative one to an authoritarian/nationalist one. Both disrespect pluralism, yet again selectively – as far as they stay on their side, "the people" are too heterogeneous to reject pluralism altogether, and are manifestly intolerant towards their own world of meanings. However, I submit that the main feature of what we tend to dub populism is, in fact, simplicism.

On simplicism

This part of the chapter is highly speculative as far as the universality of the idea is concerned, yet it collates convincing empirical evidence from Poland, warranting further test for the idea.

Briefly, as mentioned in the theoretical part on populism, the phenomenon is multidimensional and associated with many other phenomena. Some authors consider most of these phenomena to be constitutive components of populism[19].

---

[19] B. Stanley, "A New Populist Divide? Correspondences of Supply and Demand

However, I am inclined to differentiate between its "core" elements, including: 1) a call for a "strong leader" who would change the system of government entirely and introduce a new, just social order; 2) the shift in blame towards a few people, who are accused to have taken control of powers which rightfully should be exercised by the people; 3) the belief that the improvement of the people's lot is threatened by the irresponsible actions of elites.

A secondary list of associated components is as follows: (i) intolerance and disrespect for pluralism; (ii) authoritarianism; (iii) use of conspiracy theories; (iv) conviction in the failure of representative institutions; (v) anti-meritocracy; (vi) nationalism and (vii) simplicism. Simplicism has two components: 1) the belief that solving the problems a country faces is very easy: it is simply necessary to give power to those who want to do it; 2) the belief that everything in politics is either good or evil, and that the choice between the two is simple.

In short, here are the key results of my analysis:

- First, my measure of simplicism is the one that most strongly correlates with the core elements of populism (see above), much more significantly than with all the remaining elements under scrutiny, including nationalism.
- Second, simplicism correlates mostly with all the remaining elements of the broader phenomena associated with populism – authoritarianism, anti-meritocracy, and failure of representative institutions in particular (these are twice as strongly correlated with simplicism compared to the core populist phenomena).
- Third, nationalism unveils strongest links with the use of conspiracy theories, simplicism, and authoritarianism.
- Fourth, in a multivariate analysis, with "core populism" as a dependent variable, the remaining components

in the 2015 Polish Parliamentary Elections", *East European Politics and Societies and Cultures*, 2018, DOI: 10.1177/0888325418783056.

unveil more or less the same picture – the strongest direct effect is manifested by simplicism, followed by the use of conspiracy theories, the rejection of pluralism, and nationalism. The gross effects of failure of representation, anti-meritocratic attitudes, and authoritarianism is being wiped out – they do not manifest a direct effect on "core populism".

- Fifth, an analysis of the impact of the three elements of populism – its "core", simplicism, and nationalism – on the vote for what most scholars call "populist" parties (PiS and Kukiz'15) *vis à vis* mainstream liberal ones (PO and Nowoczesna) shows that in the case of PiS versus PO+N the direct effect of the "core" disappears in a multivariate regression design and with significant similar direct effects of simplism and nationalism. When Kukiz'15 is juxtaposed with PO+N, only nationalism exerts both gross and net effect, i.e., in this case, "core populism" and "simplicism" do not matter even when analysed separately.

Conclusions

Populism and nationalism are political phenomena tightly linked with each other, irrespective of the fact that the former is a *thick* ideology and the latter only a *thin* one. An overview of the CEE region's parties demonstrates that populism and nationalism display an overlap, i.e. all parties considered "populist" display a nationalist component and many of them simultaneously unveil populist elements. This Eastern European nationalism manifests itself in different forms: it almost always has an economic component; it recently acquired an anti-EU flavour; at times (though clearly less frequently) it exhibits aggressive racial or ethnic hatred oriented at minorities or ethnic groups from neighbouring countries.

The "core populist" elements – belief in the superiority of "the people", contempt for the allegedly corrupted elite, disbelief in representative institutions – are universally present as its constitutive components, but especially during electoral campaigns and/or among smaller, irrelevant parties that are unlikely to form part of governing coalitions. The rapid change with which successful political parties abandon part or most of the populist policy repertoire (even if their discourse remains populist) is visible in most instances, be it in the Bulgarian Simeon II Movement, the Polish PiS, or the Hungarian Fidesz.

Finally, nationalism is firmly linked to "core" populism, yet simplicism is definitely more so. Moreover, simplicism seems to better explain the electoral linkage between supporters and the so-called "populist" parties. So far I have presented data only for Poland and a lot of further theorising is needed to ontologically defend "simplicism" as an independent phenomenon from core populism, one that is likely to have an important impact on what happens in politics. To be sure, simplicism should be treated as a method of communication between the elites and the masses, and as a political linkage based on the assumption that the surrounding world, politics, and economy are simple. A more detailed explanation of simplicism deserves a separate paper, which hopefully will follow soon.

4. The Unsettling Shadow of the Past: National-Populism in Austria

Karin Liebhart

Austria's general election in late 2017 resulted in the formation of an overall right-wing populist coalition government led by Sebastian Kurz, leader of the centre-right, conservative ÖVP (Austrian People's Party), with the far-right FPÖ (Freedom Party of Austria) as a junior partner. Both parties had focused their election campaigns on anti-immigration policy and corresponding rhetoric, a strategy that has primarily been pursued by the Freedom Party during the last three decades. Kurz became Europe's youngest head of government. Under his leadership, the mainstream party ÖVP has admittedly altered both its policy positions and the style of political communication to meet the populist challenge. According to Anton Pelinka, the People's Party's successful election campaign consisted in "stealing talking points from the FPÖ and presenting them in more moderate garments and with better manners"[1]. The quote draws attention to an ongoing process of convergence between far-right populist and centre-right parties, at least in regard to the nationalist-populist framing of migration and asylum policy. Such developments indicate that right-wing populism and appeal to nationalist sentiments have definitely reached the political mainstream in Austria, and also society at large. How has this come about?

---

[1] P. Oltermann, "Sebastian Kurz's audacious gamble to lead Austria pays off", *The Guardian*, 15 October 2017.

A Brief History of National-Populism in Austria

Compared to other EU member states like Germany, where far-right populist parties such as AfD (Alternative for Germany) have only recently gained significant voters' support at the federal level, national-populist politics have a decades-long tradition in Austria, first and foremost represented by the Freedom Party.

Established in 1955/1956 as a successor of the VdU (Federation of Independents), a receptacle of former national socialists founded in 1949, the early Austrian Freedom Party stood for Pan-Germanism and propagated the idea that the "Austrian identity" was part of a greater German national identity. In contrast to other far-right parties like the SVP (Swiss People's Party), the Dutch Party of Freedom, or the French National Rally (formerly known as the National Front until June 2018), the Austrian Freedom Party does not belong to the so-called "New Right". The latter has no direct roots in fascist or national-socialist movements, while the FPÖ's first and second chairmen were former SS officers. Until the second half of the 1980s, the FPÖ only played a minor role in Austrian politics, except for the years 1983 to 1986 when the party, under the leadership of Norbert Steger, put forward more liberal views and served as a junior partner in a coalition government led by the SPÖ (Social Democratic Party of Austria).

The year 1986 marked a fundamental change – the end of the short liberal period and the beginning of the party's rise as a significant actor in Austrian politics. The charismatic politician Jörg Haider was elected party leader with a large majority. He instantly initiated an ideological turn and transformed the FPÖ into an explicitly right-wing populist and nationalist party, based on ideological reorientation[2]. Haider focused on immigration and integration issues – shifting, later on, especially towards anti-Muslim and anti-Islam sentiments – as well as

---

[2] Cf. A. Pelinka, "Die FPÖ in der vergleichenden Parteienforschung. Zur typologischen Einordnung der Freiheitlichen Partei Österreichs", in *Österreichische Zeitschrift für Politikwissenschaft*, no. 3/2002, pp. 281-299.

criticism of the political establishment. Moreover, the new party leader foregrounded an ethnically defined, discrete Austrian national identity instead of preaching the country's belonging to a superordinate German nation. Haider's novel topical positioning and populist rhetoric with a shifted nationalist focus on Austrian identity construction paved the way for increased electoral support[3]. Over the years, Haider and his successors made immigration the most heatedly debated political issue in Austria. In 1993, the party initiated a referendum that called for a more restrictive immigration policy under the heading "Austria First!"[4]. By the end of the 1990s, the FPÖ intensified campaigning against the alleged threat of the "Islamisation" of Austria and other European countries, and discursively linked the topic with the debate on Turkey's potential EU membership. From the turn of the millennium onwards, the Austrian Freedom Party, followed by its split-off (BZÖ - Alliance for the Future of Austria) constantly fueled the anti-Islamic climate. Simultaneously, the Freedom Party completely changed its attitude towards the European Union and started blaming the EU and Brussel's bureaucracy for every bad. This mixture of anti-immigration stances, anti-Islam/anti-Muslim rhetoric, and Euroscepticism if not hostility towards the EU led the party to striking electoral successes both at local and national level[5].

The First Right-Wing Coalition

Winning nearly 27% of the vote in the 1999 general election made the FPÖ the second strongest party after the SPÖ and brought it into government as a junior partner of the

---

[3] Cf. S. Kritzinger and K. Liebhart, Austria, in: D.M. Viola (ed.), *Handbook of European Elections*, Taylor and Francis, London, Routledge, 2015, pp. 377-395.
[4] Consequentially five FPÖ MPs, who opposed such political ideas, left the faction and founded the Liberal Forum LIF.
[5] S. Kritzinger and K. Liebhart (2015).

third-placed People's Party in 2000[6]. Though Jörg Haider was not part of the government himself, because he was seen as too controversial, the acceptance of a far-right, nationalist-populist party linked to National Socialism through its coalition partner set off significant protest on both national and international level, and the fourteen other EU members called for a diplomatic boycott. However, as a matter of fact, the FPÖ's pariah status ended in 2000.

Soon after its entrance into the coalition, the party experienced what virtually every populist anti-elite party faces when shifting from opposition to participation in government. This shift – from anti-establishment party to party in power – also implied the support of neo-liberal economic reforms that led to severe internal conflicts and party instability. The party was not able to handle the internal quarrels properly, a couple of ministers resigned, and consequently electoral support decreased significantly. When it came to general elections in 2002, the FPÖ faced a loss of nearly two-thirds of the votes compared to 1999[7]. Nevertheless, the party decided to carry forward the coalition.

Due to ongoing internal dissent, Jörg Haider, together with the deputy chancellor and all FPÖ ministers, left the party in 2005 and founded a new one, the BZÖ, which replaced the FPÖ in the coalition. In the wake of the unexpected death of Jörg Haider in a car accident in 2008, the BZÖ lost significant electoral support and did not pass the 4% threshold in the following 2013 general elections[8].

After the split, Heinz-Christian Strache was elected as new chairman of the FPÖ. By pushing well-known topics such as anti-immigration stances, anti-Muslimism, and Euroscepticism, Strache aimed at further radicalising both the party's ideology and political campaign strategies. Under his leadership, the

---

[6] Bundesministerium Inneres, http://www.bmi.gv.at/412/.
[7] Cf. C. Heinisch, "Die FPÖ – Ein Phänomen im internationalen Vergleich. Erfolg und Misserfolg des identitären Rechtspopulismus", *Österreichische Zeitschrift für Politikwissenschaft*, no. 3/2004, pp. 247-261.
[8] Bundesministerium für Inneres..., cit.

FPÖ succeeded in both state and federal elections. In 2010, for instance, it reached 25.8% of the vote share and became the second most powerful political force in Austria's capital Vienna[9]. Further electoral successes (amongst others, 20.5% in the 2013 general election, and 30.4%, in state elections in Upper Austria and 30.8% in Vienna in 2015[10]) and the acceptance as a partner in SPÖ- or ÖVP-led regional governments in Burgenland and Upper Austria additionally contributed to the definite end of the so-called "cordon sanitaire." While the 2014 European Parliament election resulted in a striking electoral success for the FPÖ (19.7%)[11], the party achieved its biggest victory in 2016, when Norbert Hofer ran for Federal Presidency on the FPÖ-ticket and won the first round with 31.1%[12]. Though Hofer was eventually defeated by the independent, Green-backed candidate Alexander Van der Bellen, he scored 49.7% and 46.2% respectively in the two run-off elections.

During all these years, the Freedom Party of Austria has presented itself as the protector of the "native Austrian people" and the ethnically-defined Austrian identity against threats allegedly imposed by both illegal immigrants (especially from Muslim countries) and the EU. Furthermore, it has always acted as a defender of social welfare for Austrian people, which according to party ideology, cannot be upheld if immigration is not strictly regulated or even completely stopped. In almost every election campaign and on all levels – local, national, and European – the FPÖ has used xenophobic slogans and images, especially against Muslims[13]. That happened before the so-called refugee crisis unfolded in 2015 and ratcheted up relevant discourses.

---

[9] Stadt Wien, https://www.wien.gv.at/wahl/NET/GR101/GR101-109.htm
[10] Bundesministerium für Inneres..., cit.
[11] European Parliament, Results of the 2014 European elections.
[12] See A. Troianovski, "European Right Gets Boost From Austrian Freedom Party Victory", *The Wall Street Journal*, 25 April 2016.
[13] Cf. F. Hafez, "Von der „Verjudung" zur „Islamistenpartei". Neue islamophobe Diskursstrategien der FPÖ im Rahmen des Wiener Wahlkampfs", in *Jahrbuch für Islamophobieforschung*, 2011, pp. 83-98.

The Freedom Party's Second Try Under Changed Framework Conditions

The most sustainable achievement of the Austrian Freedom Party is probably that its leading politicians have successfully managed to change the political discourse in Austria and reframe the political debate. The legislative elections of 2017 have shown that right-wing populist views are by now no longer limited to the fringes of the political landscape, but have directly reached the political mainstream[14].

Sebastian Kurz, who had become leader of the Austrian People's Party only about half a year before the elections took place in October last year, successfully rebranded the party into a political "movement for Austria", completely focused on him as a person. He renamed it "Sebastian Kurz List - the New People's Party", changed its color from black to turquoise, and adopted a populist style of politics and political communication. The brand "Sebastian Kurz" proved strong, and support among potential voters increased quickly and dramatically, from around 20% to 31.5% (+ 7.5% compared to 2013)[15]. Kurz called snap elections and ran the campaign under the heading of change, adopting the slogan "Time for something new". That he himself has served as a member of the previous government for more than three years was obviously not seen as contradictory by a significant number of voters.

It has to be mentioned in this regard that a very similar slogan has been used a few years earlier by the Team Stronach for Austria (TS), founded in 2012, which represents the type of so-called entrepreneurial populism, characterised by the use of marketing techniques and weak ideological orientation. The term defines a party led by a business tycoon-turned-politician

---

[14] F. Murphy, "Win or Lose, Austrian Far Right's Views Have Entered Government", Reuters, 16 July 2017.

[15] Bundesministerium für Inneres, National Council election (National Council election) 2017, https://wahl17.bmi.gv.at/

who suggests to run government like a business[16]. In the case of Austria, the party founder and its first leader was the Austrian-Canadian billionaire Frank Stronach who, during the first two years, gained between 8.3% and 11.3% in three federal elections and 5.7% in nationwide elections, attracting voters from all other parties. Team Stronach was attractive especially to those voters who felt that there is no longer any difference between the two mainstream parties SPÖ and ÖVP and it is "Time for change", particularly in regard to the rules of the political game and the alleged inefficiency of government. The success of Team Stronach did not last, mainly because of Stronach's political inexperience and misbehaviour and his ignorance of political conventions[17].

Sebastian Kurz successfully managed to leverage the Freedom party's main political topics, making immigration "his signature issue". His populist strategy, which also appealed to xenophobic feelings, paid off. He repeatedly claimed that it was him who closed down to refugees the Balkan route to Europe, called for tougher border controls, and repelled alleged activities of "political Islam"[18] in order to protect Austrian democracy and European values. Against the backdrop of widespread anti-refugee sentiment in Austria, this message was well received by the voters. Indeed, the Austrian Freedom Party, which had mostly ranked first in the polls since 2014, also polled strongly in the election and got 26% (+5.5% compared to 2013) of the votes, but only reached the third place after the Social Democrats (26.9%). However, the party leader Heinz-Christian Strache became deputy chancellor in the new coalition government, and the Freedom Party has since controlled the key departments of foreign affairs, defense, and internal affairs.

---

[16] Cf. R.C. Heinisch and St. Saxonberg, "Entrepreneurial Populism and the Radical Centre: Examples from Austria and the Czech Republic", in R.C. Heinisch, C. Holtz-Bacha, and O. Mazzoleni (eds.), *Political Populism. A Handbook*, Baden-Baden, Nomos, 2009, pp. 209-226.

[17] Ibid.

[18] P. Oltermann (2017).

The inauguration of the ÖVP - FPÖ government in December 2017 was the second time the FPÖ came to power since 2000, when the then-ÖVP chairman Wolfgang Schüssel broke the taboo of forming a coalition with the far-right nationalist Freedom Party. "Vienna Calling. A new coalition in Austria brings the far-right in from the cold" was the banner headline of the Economist on 19 December 2017[19].

This time, it seems that the Freedom Party performs better in balancing the requirements of participating in government and the expectations of party members and supporters. Recent surveys[20] suggest that the FPÖ has indeed been losing support from some of its core constituencies. However, as of September 2018, the party scores on average around 24.7% in terms of nationwide support.

The coalition government operates overall in harmony, not least enabled by the People's Party's remarkable shift to the right. Generally, the Freedom Party, the less experienced partner in power, follows the guidelines provided by the People's Party. However, discrepancies appear here and there, and the shadows of the Freedom Party's past, as well as its nationalist, far-right ideology, linger on present politics.

With regards to a core political aim of the Freedom Party, i.e., the strengthening of direct democracy tools such as plebiscites in order to weaken representative democracy, the senior coalition partner has curtailed the plans of its junior partner and postponed any decisions to the end of the legislative period[21].

Concerning economic policies, the Freedom Party overall supports the People's Party's (neo)liberal approach. This has become obvious in regard to approval of the Comprehensive Economic and Trade Agreement between the EU and Canada,

---

[19] "A new coalition in Austria brings the far right in from the cold", *The Economist*, 19 December 2017.
[20] Welche Partei würden Sie wählen, wenn am nächsten Sonntag Nationalratswahl wäre?, Das Statistik-Portal, 2018.
[21] N. Weissensteiner, *Direkte Demokratie: Hohe Hürden für Referenden bis nach 2022 garantiert*, Analysis, Der Standard, 16 December 2017.

which the FPÖ had previously strongly opposed. The Freedom Party is also basically in line with its coalition partner in the fields of social policy, and it even agreed to weaken labour laws. Almost no differences can be observed when it comes to reforms concerning family policies. Both parties share a conservative approach to this policy field.

Though the two main representatives of the coalition government, Sebastian Kurz and Heinz-Christian Strache, had assured Austrian Federal President Alexander Van der Bellen of sharing his "pro-European" perspective prior to the swearing-in ceremony, relevant concerns remain. The commitment to the European Union is, at least in the case of the Freedom Party, not fully credible given the party's particularly Eurosceptic course for years and its close alignment with other Eurosceptic parties such as Alternative for Germany and the French National Rally on the European level. However, with the ÖVP's persistent yet critical support of EU integration, the FPÖ had to compromise, especially against the background of Austria's EU presidency in the second half of 2018.

No contradictory political views can be observed in regard to the topical issue of migration. Recently, the two parties agreed on further restricting access to asylum seekers in the Austrian labour market, on cutting funds for integration initiatives such as German-language courses, and on accelerating the expulsion of undocumented immigrants from the Austrian soil. Unsurprisingly, the Freedom Party also supports chancellor Kurz's plans of building migrant processing centres in North African countries and to allow Frontex border guards to operate in the Southern neighbouring countries of the EU to prevent refugees' attempts to reach Europe via the Mediterranean Sea[22]. The decision to follow Hungary and the United States in rejecting the global migration pact and backing out of it can serve as a further example in this regard[23].

---

[22] F.-S. Gady, "Has Austria Found the Answer to Right-Wing Populism?", *Foreign Affairs*, 11 September 2018.

[23] F. Murphy, "Austria backing out of global migration pact", Reuters, 31 October 2018.

More sensitive for the stability of the governing coalition are the Internal Affairs and Justice policy fields. While the Freedom Party did not attack the independence of the judiciary so far, it tried to establish controversial personalities in both Supreme Courts of Austria. When it came to the nomination of judges for the Supreme Constitutional Court of Austria in February/March 2018, the FPÖ nominated a professor of law from the University of Linz who is member of a far-right fraternity, and had before polemicised against the European Court of Human Rights[24]. Recently, the party nominated a very controversial personality to the Supreme Administrative Court. Some years ago, this judge – who because of protests eventually decided not to run for the office – had called Franz Jägerstätter, a conscientious objector who had been executed by the NS regime for refusing to serve in the German Wehrmacht, a traitor[25].

Deputy chancellor Heinz-Christian Strache and other party members have attacked the public service broadcaster ORF and accused the institution of being left-wing biased. However, they did not succeed in reorganising the ORF fundamentally, which would be the party's eventual goal in terms of media policy[26]. Equally problematic are verbal attacks against critical journalists on the part of FPÖ politicians. The chancellor has so far remained silent in most cases.

Since the FPÖ obtained the Interior and Defense Ministries, it also controls both Austria's security apparatus and intelligence agencies. Currently, an occurrence in which the Minister of Interior, Herbert Kickl, is involved, is a matter of controversial debate. The incident concerns the Office for the Protection of the Constitution and Counterterrorism, Austria's domestic intelligence agency, and the illegal seizure of agency intelligence on right-wing extremist groups in Austria (supposedly

---

[24] Bundespräsident akzeptiert Andreas Hauer für Verfassungsgericht - derstandard, Der Standard, video, 1 March 2018.
[25] "Keyl zieht Bewerbung als Bundesverwaltungsrichter zurück", OÖNachrichten.
[26] FPÖ-Angriffe auf ORF, "Es geht um die Pressefreiheit in Österreich", 18 April 2018.

including FPÖ members) during an illegal police raid initiated by party members. This has to be seen against the background of Herbert Kickl's attempts to appoint a new head of the organisation by discrediting the incumbent one. The case is still under investigation[27].

The Shadows of the Past

While generally the FPÖ has reduced its extremist rhetoric, some more extremist members of the party like the chairmen of its parliamentary faction Johann Gudenus did not. Gudenus publicly discredited LGBTQ people and echoed anti-Semitic conspiracy theories concerning George Soros[28]. Yet, without any consequences. Herbert Kickl, the FPÖ interior minister, suggested that asylum seekers should be "concentrated" in one place, a clear nod to nazism[29].

As of recently, deputy chancellor Strache publicly rejected anti-Semitism, Holocaust denial, and racism, even during a speech delivered to a far-right audience on occasion of the controversial right-wing Academics Ball 2018. Strache continues attempt to clean up the party's image, for example by publishing a so-called "Rot-Weiss-Rot Erklärung" on the FPÖ homepage. The declaration was written with the intent to prove that the party is neither extremist nor racist nor anti-Semitic but supports the idea of an Austrian nation-state and democratic principles[30]. The party has further decided to end financial support for the extreme-right publication Aula. The Freedom Party has even built a commission of historians who investigate

---

[27]   https://www.nachrichten.at/nachrichten/politik/innenpolitik/BVT-Affaere-Goldgrubers-schwieriges-Verhaeltnis-zur-Extremismus-Ermittlerin;art385,3055623
[28] A. Thalhammer, "Gudenus und die Soros-Verschwörungen", *Die Presse*, 22 April 2018.
[29] L. Hagen, "Kickl will Flüchtlinge 'konzentriert' an einem Ort halten", Der Standard, 11 January 2018.
[30] "Rot-weiß-rote Ehrenerklärung: FPÖ gegen Antisemitismus und Extremismus", FP Die Soziale HeimatPartei, 13 February 2018.

the party's history in order to get rid of potential further issues. Though this idea was welcomed in principle, the presentation of the steering group and the leading members of the planned commission raised serious doubts about their neutrality. Some of the leading figures have close ties to Neo-Nazism and right-wing extremism[31]. The results of the commission's investigation are not yet available. Anyway, Strache has also been criticised by FPÖ party members and various far-right "alternative" media outlets for his compliance with mainstream politics.

According to a study compiled by the Austrian Mauthausen Committee, cases of anti-Semitism, racism, and homophobia have, nevertheless, increased since the FPÖ entered government in December 2017[32]. A closer look to the domestic political arena reveals that the acceptance of the FPÖ as a coalition partner has already caused a couple of political troubles since the inauguration of the current government. In particular, the important role which members of far-right students' fraternities (Burschenschaften) play now in government and parliament and in other institutions of the Republic of Austria as well is reason to concern[33]. Many of these mostly sexist and far-right fraternities still uphold anti-Semitic and xenophobic attitudes. Some of them also deny that Austria is a nation of its own and claim a sense of belonging to a "Greater Germany". Former candidate for the presidential election in 2016 and current minister of transport and infrastructure, Norbert Hofer, is still member of a fraternity called Marko-Germania. The founding document of the latter terms Austria after 1945 a "history-defying

---

[31] Cf. H.-H. Scharsach, "Personal der FPÖ – HISTORIKERKOMMISSIONH mit Neonazis verstrick", empoerteuch.at, 13 February 2018.
[32] C.M. Schmidt, "Broschüre dokumentiert FPÖ-Skandale", Der Standard, 22 August 2017.
[33] These student organizations are for men only. They propagate a particular outdated understanding of maleness, organize fencing duels among members of the relevant fraternity and show their dueling scars openly. Wearing a uniform unique to the fraternity on official occasions completes the picture (http://www.dw.com/en/inside-the-secretive-fraternities-of-germany-and-austria/a-42447338).

fiction"[34]. Remarkable high numbers of FPÖ politicians, including party leader Heinz-Christian Strache and a couple of the party's chairmen, have close bonds with far-right student fraternities. Out of the party's 51 members of parliament, more than a third (18) are active members of right-wing to extreme right fraternities[35]. Recently, Udo Landbauer, one of the top candidates of the Austrian Freedom Party for the elections in the province of Lower Austria and deputy co-chairman of the fraternity Germania zu Wiener Neustadt, eventually had to resign after the weekly newspaper Falter had drawn attention to a songbook which was reissued in 1993 and used by the fraternity. This songbook comprises anti-Semitic songs and praises the NS Wehrmacht. The Falter had published an excerpt of one of these songs which "celebrated atrocities committed by the Wehrmacht and mocked Holocaust victims"[36]. Currently, Landbauer is back in politics, since the investigations did not deliver any hard proof that he did not tell the truth while asserting that he personally did not know about the incriminating pages in the songbook.

Since it quickly turned out that the fraternity Germania zu Wiener Neustadt is not the only far-right fraternity adopting songbooks that contain anti-Semitic and racist songs[37], the FPÖ leader Strache stated that "antisemitism, totalitarianism (and) racism are the opposite of fraternity thinking" and have no place in the party. Moreover, he argued that "(F)raternities have nothing to do with the FPÖ"[38].

This sounds surprising, since far-right fraternities are also the organizers of the so-called Academics Ball which traditionally takes place in the Viennese Hofburg, one of the

---

[34] P. Oltermann, "Austria's far-right fraternities brace for protests at annual ball", *The Guardian*, 25 January 2018.

[35] C.M. Schmidt and F. Schmid, "Bünde fürs Leben: FPÖ-Minister vertrauen auf Burschenschafter", 26 January 2018.

[36] P. Oltermann, "Austria's far-right fraternities brace for protests at annual ball"…, cit.

[37] Cfr."Neue Liederbuch-Affäre", *Kleine Zeitung*, 21 February 2018.

[38] P. Oltermann, "Austria to dissolve Nazi songbook fraternity linked to Freedom party", *The Guardian*, 1 February 2018.

most representative official buildings of the Austrian state. The Academics Ball is a highly controversial event, attended every year by key FPÖ representatives, which always goes along with civil society protests and demonstrations, since it also functions as a meeting place for right-wing populist and right-wing extremist politicians from a number of European countries[39].

Conclusions

The Freedom Party is stuck in third place since entering into a coalition government with the People's Party, despite having a relatively stable support of nearly 25% of votes in the polls. This is certainly remarkable, since the party had to make many compromises during the last year. A lot of them definitely disappointed FPÖ supporters. Nevertheless, the outlook is more promising for the FPÖ than it used to be 18 years earlier. The fact that the senior coalition partner, the New People's Party, has significantly shifted to the right has definitely contributed to make life easier for the FPÖ.

Recently, the journal Foreign Affairs raised the question of whether the integration of the far-right Freedom Party and its representatives in key political positions in the government has turned Austria into a more Eurosceptic and anti-immigration country, aligning more closely to countries such as Poland and Hungary.[40] Overall, the picture remains ambivalent. The answer is probably that such tendencies are observable, but not due to the influence of the Freedom Party alone. The main cause, in fact, is the general shift to the right in Austrian politics.

This development is echoed by similar processes in other European countries as well. The fact that the announcement of the establishment of the coalition between the "Sebastian Kurz

---

[39] Ibid.

[40] F.-S. Gady, "Has Austria Found the Answer to Right-Wing Populism?", *Foreign Affairs*, 11 September 2018.

List" and the far right-wing populist Austrian Freedom Party in December 2017 hardly caused any protests by other EU member states or other countries can be seen as an indicator in this regard. It seems that the inclusion of the far right has become so normal that the Austrian case is no longer perceived as exceptional, and thus it has not faced any remarkable sign of political quarantine. This stands in sharp contrast to what happened in the year 2000, when diplomatic reactions were quick and bilateral meetings, state visits, and diplomatic encounters were frozen. After the 2017 general elections, Austria has eventually become the symbol of a wider trend.

Meanwhile, the political mainstream has gone populist, with nationalist tendencies. This can be considered a success of the far-right, which impacted on both the political discourse and factual politics. Concerning Austria, the FPÖ may still be called the epitome of anti-immigrant and especially anti-Muslim stances, but related populist-national rhetoric has by now become so normalised that representatives of other parties also make use of it. Hence, it can be assumed that the FPÖ has first and foremost achieved an ideological victory. Both the ÖVP under the leadership of Sebastian Kurz and also some groups within the SPÖ have turned significantly to the right, adopting an FPÖ-like rhetoric style, and also promoting political ideas originally introduced by the Freedom Party. Thus, mainstream parties often act as lite versions of the FPÖ.

Today, anti-pluralistic tendencies have become more and more apparent in Austrian society, while pluralistic political concepts and strategies that seek to establish frames for discussing and managing differences are increasingly under attack. According to Ruth Wodak, the Europe-wide swing towards anti-establishment parties has normalised right-wing populist political stances, especially in terms of more restrictive immigration policies and correspondent offensive rhetoric: "Some of the policies that right-wing populists have endorsed have already been taken over and implemented. (...) Certain taboos have been broken and now it's seemingly okay to say certain very discriminatory things, even without a big scandal." Wodak continues: "The levels have lowered of taboos and conventions, normalisation is on its way"[41].

---

[41]   http://www.euronews.com/2018/03/15/explained-the-rise-and-rise-of-populism-in-europe.

5. Turkey's AKP and the West: Nationalism, Populism and Beyond

Ilke Toygür

Understanding Turkish politics have been a puzzling task in the last decade. For many observers, Turkey has changed very quickly from a textbook rising economy and a Muslim democracy to a consolidating authoritarian regime. Even if its democracy has always been defined as a "tutelary democracy", the deterioration was still very sharp. According to the Freedom House's "Freedom in the World" report, Turkey has declined from "partly free" to "not free" in 2018 for violations of basic rights and freedoms in the country[1]. The state of emergency declared in the aftermath of the failed coup attempt in July 2016 contributed to this decline. In this context, both the constitutional referendum and the most critical snap election that would complete the transformation to a presidential system took place. The Organization for Security and Co-operation in Europe (OSCE) reports on elections clearly stated the "unfair playing ground" and questioned if both the referendum and the election fulfilled the requirements of democratic competition[2].

Even if this is the case, President Recep Tayyip Erdoğan and his AKP (Justice and Development Party) claimed electoral legitimacy and named these elections' results "*the nation's will*". The concept of democracy for the party's elites is mainly based on voting in elections and do not take into account other

---

[1] Freedom in the World 2018, Turkey Profile, Freedom House, 2018.
[2] Elections in Turkey, OSCE, 2018.

fundamentals of a functioning democracy such as a strong rule of law or basic rights and freedoms. For them, parliamentary majority is the unique source of legitimacy, while the idea of separation of powers is constantly undermined. This understanding of the vote as the main demonstration of the "will of the people", while failing to taking the opposition voters' preferences into account opened the door to a polarisation of the country, harming the pluralism in society. Meanwhile, the supporters of the government were referred to as "real citizens" of Turkey, while the other half as "terrorists" or "enemies of the nation".

Taking all this into account, the AKP has been included in the list of populist parties in Europe. Differently from its European counterparts, though, the party governed since its establishment, and it has never been in the opposition. Its winning narrative has been based on challenging the existing ruling elite – founders of the Republic, the military and the judiciary – and restructuring the society[3]. Akkoyunlu and Öktem (2016) underlined in their article that the AKP government constantly undermined the checks and balances in the system, solely underlining the participation in elections as the unique demonstration of the level of democracy in the country. The main cleavage of Turkish society, the centre-periphery[4], opened the floor to the AKP's populist strategy and discourse. Not only did the AKP mobilise the masses and restructure the ruling elite, but it also changed the constitution significantly. After

---

[3] Two articles would enrich the understanding of the reader: K. Akkoyunlu and K. Öktem, "Existential insecurity and the making of a weak authoritarian regime in Turkey", *Southeast European and Blacksea Studies*, vol. 16, no. 4, 2016; B. Çelik and E. Balta, "Explaining the micro dynamics of the populist cleavage in the 'new Turkey'", *Mediterranean Politics*, 2018.

[4] Şerif Mardin argued that the Turkish society has a central divide which is inherited from the Ottoman Empire. The divide is formed by the ruling elite of the "centre" and culturally heterogeneous "periphery". The full formulation can be found in S. Mardin, "Centre-periphery relations: A key to Turkish politics?", *Daedalus*, 1973.

two constitutional referendums in 2007 and 2010[5], a third referendum in 2017 and an election in 2018, converted Turkey into a presidential system *à la Turca*.

Last but not least, the AKP's populist rule and rising nationalism in Turkey could not be understood without discussing the country's geographical location, its foreign policy and its troubled relationships with its Western allies. In addition to anti-elitism and polarisation in the society, the instrumentalisation of the West and blame-shifting is an important part of the AKP's discourse. For this reason, this chapter will first go through the electoral history of the AKP, move to the constitutional referendum that changed the system in Turkey and then analyse the election that introduced these changes. As a complementary part of the puzzle, the article will provide a history of Turkey's relations with the West to shed light on how nationalism plays a crucial role in the country. This chapter will also question whether the Turkish case is setting the ground and the tone for illiberalism in Europe. Finally, it will present conclusions and provide policy recommendations.

The AKP and Its Electoral History

Turkey's ruling party, the AKP was founded in 2001 by the reformist wing of the Welfare Party (RP). Back then, Turkey was in the middle of an economic crisis and facing a collapse of its coalition government, formed by the centre-left Democratic Left Party (DSP), the Nationalist Movement Party (MHP) and the centre-right Motherland Party (ANAP), thus including a wide spectrum of the political scene. When citizens attributed the blame of the economic crisis to the government, centrist

---

[5] The AKP has been changing the constitution slowly but steadily from the very beginning. It broght the military and the judiciary under control, removing their privileges. It introduced the direct election of the president, opening the way to the politicisation of the post. Throughout its mandate, consensus building in the Parliament was replaced by majorities supported by the popular vote.

political parties lost popular support. In the populism literature such conditions are listed as factors leading to the emergence of populist parties[6]. Once significant parties on the centre of the political spectrum were crushed, the necessary political space for the rise of a new political party was created. The AKP was born.

The AKP, from the very beginning of its mandate, exploited the primary cleavage in Turkish politics, which is the centre-periphery divide. It structured its discourse against the centralist, secular elite that controlled the state apparatus since 1923 and defended the conservative masses of the periphery. Clearly, this was not the first attempt to challenge the ruling elite – owner of the state apparatus – in Turkey. The top-down modernisation and Westernisation of the country caused reactions and had representatives in the system since the introduction of multiparty elections in 1946. However, every previous attempt had been stopped by the military before it became significantly powerful[7]. First it was the DP (Democratic Party) – that won the first free and fair elections in 1950 mobilising the periphery. In the post-1960 era, the AP (Justice Party) has also emerged as the party that represents the conservative masses. After the 1980s, both the ANAP and the DYP (True Path Party) structured themselves as the representatives of "the people". In addition to the ANAP and the DYP, the National Outlook Movement (*Milli Görüş*) with its Islamist ideology took over some of the political space in Turkey. Many of the AKP's founding leaders come from the National Outlook Movement itself. The main discourse of these parties and movements has always been similar: to represent the people against the elite of the country; an elite that forced a top-down modernisation through the decades and controlled the state since the foundation of the Republic.

---

[6] C. Mudde, "The Populist Zeitgeist", *Government and Opposition*, vol. 39, no. 4, 2004, pp. 541-63; and C.R. Kaltwasser, "The ambivalence of populism: Threat or corrective for democracy", *Democratization*, vol. 19, no. 1, 2012, pp. 184-208.

[7] In Turkey, the military intervened in politics with different tools in 1960, 1971 (Memorandum), 1980, 2007 (E-Memorandum) and 2017 (failed coup attempt).

Following the entry of the AKP into the political scene in 2001, the country went to the polls in November 2002 following the collapse of the aforementioned coalition government, and the AKP secured an electoral majority with 34% of the popular vote. It got almost two-thirds of the seats[8] and started a new epoch in Turkish politics. Its majority survived both in 2007 and 2011. The wind changed in the June 2015 election, when the AKP lost its parliamentary majority and Turkey got its most pluralistic parliament in a long time. However, coalition talks failed, and the governing party managed to call a snap election in November 2015, regaining its majority. With this experience in mind, the AKP elite was convinced that to maintain their rule the country needed a system change. That desired change would come in just three years, making the party's leader one of the most powerful leaders in the history of the country.

While the political party is discussed in detail, its leader Recep Tayyip Erdoğan should be named right from the very beginning. Erdoğan started as Prime Minister[9] and ended up being the first elected President of the Republic under the parliamentary system in 2014. Following the 2017 referendum and 2018 election, he solidified his rule and converted Turkey into a presidential system *à la Turca*. This could be named as one of the most complete transformations a political party has ever achieved. For this reason, this chapter will go through the constitutional referendum and the election that introduced the new system. In addition, it will focus on Turkey's relationship with the broader West to analyze the blame-shifting discourse

---

[8] The main reason behind the disproportional distribution of seats in the Parliament is the extremely high threshold in Turkey. The 10% threshold was introduced in 1983, after the 1980 *coup d'état*, aiming to keep various political parties out while decreasing the fragmentation in the Parliament. The 2002 election has been a case book example of how such a high threshold can lead to a Parliament that is failing to represent millions of citizens.

[9] As previously mentioned, Recep Tayyip Erdoğan started his political career in the National Outlook Movement. Before becoming the leader of AKP and Prime Minister of the country, he also served as the mayor of Istanbul.

of the government, which enforces nationalism in the country. The AKP's success cannot be fully understood without mentioning the role played by nationalism.

The New Constitution of the New Turkey: The April 2017 Referendum and Beyond

The 2017 constitutional reform brought about the most significant political changes since the establishment of the Republic of Turkey in 1923 and its shift to multiparty politics in 1946. The core of the proposal has focused on the position of the president, previously primarily symbolic and serving as a checks and balances mechanism, which became fully executive as the Head of State and Government. The president is elected directly by the Turkish citizens for a maximum period of two terms of five years each[10], and he can lead a political party. Thus, the figure of an impartial president disappeared: the post has been politicised. The 2017 reform process was designed as a change from a parliamentary regime to a presidential one, granting the president the role of selecting ministers and appointing the Cabinet, while drastically diminishing the supervisory rights of the parliament. In addition to this sharp turn, the number of deputies has increased from 550 to 600, while the age limit to become a deputy is reduced from 25 to 18. Even if those were welcomed moves to increase the representation of the Parliament, the overall lack of influence of the body made these changes just symbolic, while increasing the public cost of the institution. In addition, the frequency of parliamentary elections changed from four to five years and the new Constitution scheduled them together with the presidential elections. This situation mostly secured that both the president and the biggest group in the Parliament will belong to the same political party. Furthermore, the president can also appoint four members of the Council of

---

[10] In case of snap elections before the term ends, the president may run again for a third term as well.

Judges and Prosecutors (HSK), while another seven would be elected by the Parliament, also currently controlled by the president's party. The Venice Commission of the Council of Europe expressed its concerns about the political regime that resulted from the implementation of this Constitution focusing on the rule of law, democracy and human rights and the existence of an independent judiciary[11].

In order to introduce the system as early as possible, the Turkish parliament called for snap elections in June 2018. There were three main reasons behind this decision. First, the economy was deteriorating and the AKP wanted to get this done before a significant economic crisis could hit. Today, looking at the economic situation, it should be said that it played really well. Second, thanks to the operations in Syria there had been an increase in nationalism that favoured the government at a time when the opposition was not at all ready. In addition, the state of emergency declared after the attempted coup in 2016 continued, making the control of protests and campaigns a lot easier. With this election, Turkish President Recep Tayyip Erdoğan fulfilled his electoral dream. Not only he won the presidential election with 52.5% of the votes in the first round, but converted the country into a presidential system that was designed by him and his party. In this context, the opposition has played its role much better than expected: the main opposition candidate, Muharrem İnce, won 31% of the vote, followed by the leftist Kurdish leader Selahattin Demirtaş, who received 8.4% of the cast ballots, and the leader of the new centre-right nationalist party, Meral Akşener (the only woman in the election), with 7.3%. This panorama once again confirmed the results of the 2017 referendum: Turkey is a divided and very polarised country, and each bloc remains in its bubble, opening the way to the populist politics of "us" versus "them".

---

[11] The full opinion on the amendments to the Constitution adopted by the Grand National Assembly on 21 January 2017, http://www.venice.coe.int/webforms/documents/default.aspx?pdffi

According to the preliminary report of the OSCE, "the voters made a genuine choice", but as it was clearly indicated "the elections were not entirely fair"[12]. The main reason for this statement is the control of the media, because almost all mainstream media are in the hands of businessmen close to the Government. According to the Press Freedom Index of Reporters Without Borders, Turkey ranks 157th out of 180 countries[13]. This has created an echo chamber around the AKP and its leader making it impossible for the opposition to reach out to its voters. If we add the state of emergency and the use of state resources (at the national and local levels) in favour of the incumbent's election campaign, the election was even more unfair. Even if this was the case, because of the very high participation rate, around 86%, the election was deemed "very democratic" and once again claimed to represent the will of the nation. Following the election, Turkey entered a new phase.

The reasons behind this success have been discussed widely by Turkey observers. These analyses share a common point: the role of rising nationalism. With the intensification of military operations and the fall of confidence in historical allies and in Western institutions, Turkish nationalism plays a very important role in electoral decisions. This issue connects national politics to international relations. Without factoring in Turkey's geography and its history with its transatlantic allies, the picture cannot be complete.

---

[12] The statement of preliminary findings and conclusions is available at: https://www.osce.org/odihr/elections/turkey/385671?download=true

[13] The Turkish casekish case is setting the ground and the tone for other strong illiberals in Europe. Shar more information regarding the index and its methodology is available at: https://rsf.org/en

Instrumentalisation of the West and Nationalism in Turkey

Turkey has been an important part of the US-led "democratisation of the world" project. Because of its geographical location and its position, during the Cold War and its aftermath the country has been a strategic partner. The existence of a liberal order in the country, a functioning free-market economy, and its European future have been supported by the United States. Counting on the transatlantic support, the elite of the Turkish Republic decided that the country belonged in Europe. This idea positioned Turkey alongside its Western allies: the country is a member of the NATO, the Council of Europe, the Union for the Mediterranean, and a candidate state for the European Union. The "Westernisation of Turkey" was an important project to strengthen the liberal world order against the Soviet Union. The post-Cold War period was also used to link Turkey to the West. This was the case both for the European Union – establishing a Customs Union – and also for the United States – increasing foreign policy cooperation.

Then the picture changed. Even if Turkey is still connected to Europe and the United States in key areas of foreign policy, such as irregular migration management, energy security, or the fight against terrorism, the relationship is very much shaped by a crisis discourse. It is expected to continue to be so for the foreseeable future even after the inception of Turkey's new presidential system *à la Turca*. The impact of this system is yet to be assessed: however, according to the governing party's declarations, in foreign policy matters Turkey foresees to collaborate not only with its Western allies but also with Russia, Iran, and China[14]. This "new" foreign policy, which has been announced in detail in the AKP's election manifesto is the reflection of what has been happening for the last years. Even though the governing elite decided

---

[14] Murat Yeşiltaş explains the key points in what he calls the "neo-realist" foreign policy. M. Yeşiltaş, "Türkiye Merkezli Yeni Dış Politika" ("Turkey centred new foreign policy"), *Setav*, 12 May 2018.

to diversify its foreign policy, it kept on politicising Turkey's relationship with the West for domestic consumption. In addition to this instrumentalisation, there is a constant blame-shifting. Every crucial challenge the government has faced – be it the Gezi Park uprisings or the corruption scandals in 2013, the coup attempt in 2016, or the economic deterioration in 2018 – was called a "plot" against its existence and "the West" was blamed.

For decades, the troubled relationship between Turkey and the European Union have contributed to this blame-shifting narrative. In particular, the never-getting-better candidacy to the European Union is the primary source of disappointment for many. If we follow Turkey's journey to join the EU, Turkey submitted its candidacy to be an associate member of the European Economic Community (EEC) in 1959, just after the EEC's creation through the Treaty of Rome in 1957. At the time, thanks to the Cold War mentality and the US's constant support, the country had been welcomed. In 1963, the EEC signed the Association Treaty with the Turkish state, i.e., the Ankara Agreement. In 1999, Turkey was accepted as a candidate country, and negotiations began in 2005. However, Turkey's candidacy always hit bumps in the road. With the membership of Greece in 1981 and Cyprus in 2004, problematic bilateral relations became a problem for EU-Turkey relations. That is why, in 2005, it was stressed that "the negotiations would be open-ended and they would not guarantee membership". A year later, in December 2006, the European Council decided that "eight chapters could not be opened and that none could be closed until Turkey accepted a full and non-discriminatory compliance with the Additional Protocol to the Association Agreement". The protocol made it necessary to open ports and airports to Cyprus – an EU member country. In addition, France and Cyprus also decided to block some chapters, damaging the real possibility of advancing in the process. In total, 16 out of 35 negotiation chapters were opened and only one was provisionally closed before the process was halted and got unofficially frozen.

Beyond the normative relationship, economic relations also followed an official path. The agreement on the Customs Union between Turkey and the European Union came into force in December 1995. In 1996, a free-trade area was established. This was not only a free-trade agreement but also an alignment of Turkish legislation with Community regulations on the internal market. Until recently, the modernisation of the Customs Union was perceived as the only option to have a relationship with standards. Both sides wanted to renegotiate it, even if that option is currently on hold because of the overall state of the relationship.

Until today, none of the parts dared to step back from the table. However, Turkey recently shut down its Ministry for EU Affairs in the context of its move towards the new presidential system. Today, the relationship is in a deadlock, and accession negotiations are practically frozen. However, Turkey and the European Union continue their transactional relationship on a less visible track. This track is mainly based on the economy, migration, border management, foreign fighters, and energy dialogue. One fact is clear: Turkey and the European Union have to come to a functioning relationship since they are neighbours and they share various challenges in the region. It is clear that Turkey is a very important ally for both sides of the Atlantic, and also a strategic ally for NATO.

Is the Turkish Case Setting the Scene for the Future?

When we look at the last two years in world politics, we see that the United Kingdom voted for Brexit, the electorate in the United States chose Donald Trump for the most powerful political post in the world, and significant democratic backsliding both in the European Union and NATO became way more visible. Autocratic tendencies and nationalism made a strong comeback on both sides of the Atlantic, and more worryingly, it looks like they are here to stay. These challenges go deep down to the roots of liberal democracy, creating a growing uncertainty for the future.

The Turkish case should be assessed as a possible lessons for other countries where liberal democracy is at stake. It is clear that Turkish history presents various drivers that are country-specific. However, there are substantial similarities between president Erdoğan and other strong illiberal leaders of the world[15]. The relationship between president Trump and president Erdoğan, for example, sets the scene. The uncertainty of their foreign policy decisions worries their allies in the world. First of all, sharing the same strategy of America-first & Turkey-first, the two biggest NATO armies are causing a good amount of uncertainty for the future. Secondly, Trump's attitude about the future of transatlantic relations is inflaming an already hostile state of relations. Together with the trade wars that have already started, the situation is not very promising. Thirdly, Turkey is one of the biggest countries in the alliance experiencing such a clear democratic backsliding. Even if this is the case, it did not necessarily face any consequences within NATO. The behaviour of the leading NATO leaders encourages other strongmen to follow. This is normalising illiberalism while polarising the alliance into two camps: the Western supporters of liberal order on the one side, the strongmen of the alliance on the other.

The European Union, on the other hand, has its own internal challenges. Hungarian Prime Minister Victor Orbán and Italian Deputy Prime Minister and Interior Minister Matteo Salvini are taking the lead. The forthcoming European Parliament elections will witness a full force implementation of populist narratives. The Union – mostly the European Parliament – is slowly considering sanctions for Hungary for democratic backsliding in the country. However, it will take quite a long time to process such decisions. For this reason, these leaders are getting

---

[15] In a recent article, Amanda Sloat listed various similarities between President Trump and President Erdoğan and they are very striking. A. Sloat, "When strongmen fight: The US and Turkey need diplomats to resolve their leaders' dispute", Brookings, 18 September 2018.

stronger and do not hesitate to use some pages from the Turkish president's playbook. The attack on the independence of the judiciary and free media in Hungary and Poland are just some examples of the deteriorating democracy in those countries.

Conclusions

This paragraph summarises the path of the AKP in Turkey. By taking advantage of the primary social cleavage in the country, the centre-periphery, the party used a populist strategy and nationalist discourse to mobilise its voters. In addition to governing for the last sixteen years, it also converted the country into a presidential system with various constitutional reforms through the years. The impact of this system is yet to be assessed; however, it is clear that it lacks the usual checks and balances and centralises the power in one person. We must also take into account that president Erdoğan will be safe in his position because the anticipation of presidential elections requires the vote of two-thirds of the members of the parliament, a scenario that is unlikely since the AKP and its coalition partner MHP holds the majority. Still, the overheating of the economy and a possible recession with high inflation – stagflation – may disrupt the status-quo. Even if this were the case, on the way to this presidential system *a la Turca* the opposition has been weakened, the judiciary's independence has been challenged, and the media have been silenced. The polarisation in the country is making it very difficult to co-exist.

So, what should European decision-makers do? How should they handle populism in Turkey, and in the rest of Europe? First of all, the roots of the existing resentment in the society that leads to the success of populists should be defined clearly. Are they primarily economic? Are they cultural? Or, like in the case of Turkey, are there any historical and structural causes that lead populist parties to emerge? It is clear that every case has its country-specific factors. However, there is a common strategy to mobilise voters: concoct a crisis. Be it cultural or economic, the socio-economic frustration bolsters populist leaders. The perception of a crisis and a common "enemy" to blame for it help the formulation of a populist narrative. This should be taken into consideration.

Secondly, it is clear that neoliberal globalisation led to a good share of the aforementioned resentment. The real connection between globalisation and the problems that are puzzling citizens today should be dismantled. Even if losers of globalisation have been thought of as the electoral base of populist parties, this is not always the case. Instead of formulating a one-fits-all description, every specific case should be studied. Mainstream political parties should offer ideological solutions to problems related to globalisation in each country, instead of trying to counter this anti-globalisation discourse.

Thirdly, objective facts matter, and they should be conveyed to the society. For this reason, every country needs free media, which is not the case in Turkey. With advancements in technology and the popularity of social media, fake news and disinformation have become very challenging problems. Still, both national governments and the European Union as a whole should work on common strategies to open the way to an independent flow of information.

Fourthly and most importantly, mainstream political parties, or any other liberal democratic ones, should stop shaping their discourse according to their populist counterparts. The clear victory of populist parties is not always governing, but mainly changing the issue space in the country. For this reason, mainstream political parties should not react to the issues that are put on the table. They should regain the power to set the tone and direct the public debate. This clearly involves providing realistic solutions to already existing problems in the society.

As a final case-specific recommendation, Turkey and its Western allies should work on their relationship. It is clear that Turkey's historical allies provide the perfect ground for blame-shifting. The blame for any challenge that the government faces goes to the "external enemy" and "the West". The main reason behind this easy blame-shifting is the current state of relations. Both the European Union and the United States should look for an honest and functioning platform to reshape their relations. Even if the transactional cooperation continues, the constant crisis discourse harms the relationship and opens the way to constant instrumentalisation.

6. National-Populism in Russia: Ticking All the Boxes?

Eleonora Tafuro Ambrosetti

Is Putin's Russia populist? The question has long preoccupied the literature on Russia's politics, generating contrasting views. Some scholars claim that Russia's government is populist[1]. Others, though, take a more moderate stance. Oliker, for instance, stresses the difference between Putinism and populism, saying that it is incorrect to blur the boundaries between the two[2]. Robinson and Milne claim that, despite the adoption of some populist themes, Putin's government is not populist[3]. While the literature is divided, nowadays it seems that Russia's populist credentials are almost given for granted by many journalists and politicians alike, who stress how Russia is becoming a model for European populists[4]. The question, however, deserves to be analysed critically. To what extent can Putin's government

---

[1] Trump Twitter Archive 2018. See, for instance, M.S. Fish, "What Has Russia Become? Comparative Politics", vol. 50, no. 3, 2018, pp. 327-46; Idem, "What Is Putinism?", *Journal of Democracy*, vol. 28, no. 4, 2017, pp. 14-29; P. Casula, "Sovereign Democracy, Populism, and Depoliticization in Russia", *Problems of Post-Communism*, vol. 60, no. 3, 2013, pp. 3-15.

[2] O. Oliker, "Putinism, Populism and the Defence of Liberal Democracy", *Survival*, vol. 59, no. 1, 2017, pp. 7-24, cit. p. 7.

[3] N. Robinson and S. Milne, "Populism and political development in hybrid regimes: Russia and the development of official populism", *International Political Science Review*, vol. 38, no. 4, 2017, pp. 412-25.

[4] A. Polyakova and P. Krekó, "Will Populist Leaders Make Voters Love Putin?", *American Interest*, 2 January 2017.

be called populist? How does this strand of populism, if present, engage with nationalism? The fuzzy nature of the concept of populism and its interaction with nationalism indeed render its application to the Russian case more complex, because it is not straightforward to call Putin's Russia "nationalist", either.

In this chapter, I argue that Putin's government, although it cannot be defined as populist or nationalist *stricto sensu,* shows indeed some populist and nationalist traits that may appeal to nationalists and populists in Europe. First, I will explore the complex relation of Putin's government with populism and nationalism. To systematise my analysis on such entangled and multifaceted concepts, I explore two cross-cutting dimensions of populism: the internal/external dimension, which, in turn, interact with the party/leader dichotomy. I then analyse the interaction between populism and nationalism in Russia's politics – especially in light of growing tensions with the West – focusing on three narratives employed by the Kremlin: the defence of compatriots, Western Russophobia, and the defence of conservative values. The conclusion puts forward some ideas on why European nationalists and populists often point at Putin as a role model, and what the EU should do about it.

"Us vs Them": The Internal Dimension

Anti-elitism is a crucial aspect of the definition of populism. According to this volume's editor, populism's ideological core is thin but at the same time very strong, since it entails a "fundamental opposition between the people and the elite, both as undifferentiated wholes, without internal rifts, conflicts of interest, different identities and loyalties"[5]. Generally, populism can be described as an "attempt to divide the political space into two camps"[6]. Applying this concise definition to Russia's domestic context means looking for an "enemy from within", an elitist group that, according to the

---

[5] A. Martinelli, *Beyond Trump: Populism on the Rise*, Milan, Epoké-ISPI, 2016, p. 15.
[6] P. Casula (2013), p. 7.

political discourse, threatens Russians' wellbeing and interests.

Russia's recent history makes the connection between elites and oligarchs straightforward for Russians and Westerners alike. Oligarchs are a by-product of the privatisation of state companies after the fall of the USSR. Russians generally maintain a negative view of them, believing them guilty of stealing the country's resources during the chaotic decade of the 1990s. However, Putin never really adopted a black-and-white "us VS them" position against the oligarchs. Rather, he curtailed their efforts and capacity to carry out autonomous political action, while co-opting them into his power architecture. A watershed moment during Putin's first year into power (2000) was indeed when he met 21 prominent oligarchs and warned them that their political power needed to come to an end. He proposed them an agreement: align with me or stay out of politics, and you can keep your fortunes or become even richer. In other words, actions against the oligarchs were not developed into an antagonistic framework, but rather as an effort to achieve a "managed normalisation", which "involved putting political, social and economic actors in their 'right' […] place, rather than defining them and defeating them as 'enemies of the people'"[7]. Only oligarchs who rebelled against this order of things or posed a threat to Putin's power faced political discrimination, seizure of assets and/or jail. Recently, the selective anti-oligarch narrative has even turned into a *tout-court* negation of the very existence of oligarchs. In the wake of another round of US sanctions against Russia last April, Kremlin spokesperson Dmitry Peskov declared that "It's been a long time since Russia had oligarchs. There are no oligarchs in Russia"[8]. While this could display an official attempt to legitimise the "organic" oligarchs, only 3% of the population bought into this narrative, according to a poll by state pollster Vtsiom.[9]

---

[7] N. Robinson and S. Milne (2017), p. 416.

[8] Кремль на фоне данных о новых санкциях США заявил об отсутствии олигархов (The Kremlin on the background of data on new US sanctions announced the absence of oligarchs), РБК, 5 April 2017.

[9] R. Abramovich "3% of Russians Agree With Kremlin That There Are 'No

At this point, it also becomes necessary to mark a sharp demarcation between the leader (Putin) and his own party (United Russia, or UR). It is possible to say that Putin has at times adopted a populist, anti-elitist stance against his own party. UR – by far the largest political party in Russia – was created exclusively to support Putin. And yet Putin did not hesitate to leave it behind when he considered that UR's decreasing popularity would harm his image. Even more, Putin seems to treat UR "more as a necessary nuisance than as an asset"[10]. Despite winning the 2016 parliamentary election, the party has indeed seen its popularity decrease and, in July, it hit its lowest levels of support since 2011, i.e. 34%[11]. In the March 2018 presidential election, Putin ran as an independent candidate in an attempt to gain more popular support. This strategy, already adopted in the 2004 presidential election, caters to the need to detach the image of the President from that of the party. Generally, Russian citizens highly distrust parties and other political institutions, seeing them as protecting the interests of some influential groups (oligarchs, corrupt officials) to the detriment of citizens[12]. Polls confirm this attitude: in 2017, only 19% of Russians had complete confidence in political parties and 27% did the same for local authorities; in comparison, 75% of respondents fully trusted the President[13]. The image of Putin as a good president, close to the needs of the people but misled by greedy and corrupt bureaucrats, is indeed widespread in Russia and is a crucial component of Putin's popularity. The "Direct Line" (Прямая линия с Владимиром Путиным), the annual special TV Q&A show with the President, is a case in point.

Oligarchs in Russia"', *The Moscow Times*, 2 Aprile 2018.

[10] M.S. Fish, "What Is Putinism?", *Journal of Democracy*, vol. 28, no. 4, October 2017 p. 69.

[11] https://wciom.ru/news/ratings/elektoralnyj_rejting_politicheskix_partij/

[12] A.J. Secor and J. O'Loughlin, "Social and Political Trust in Istanbul and Moscow: A Comparative Analysis of Individual and Neighbourhood Effects", *Transactions of the Institute of British Geographers*, vol. 30, no. 1, 2005, pp. 66-82, p. 79.

[13] https://www.levada.ru/2017/10/12/institutsionalnoe-doverie-3/?fromtg=1

The hours-long show displays a benevolent president that listens to the populace's grievances and, often, fixes problems created by inefficient and corrupt administrators, similar to the initial format of "Hello Mr President" (*Aló Presidente*) hosted by former Venezuelan President Hugo Chávez.

Hence, is Putin a populist leader? Again, a nuanced view is preferable. There are at least two features of Putin's governing style that differentiate him from leaders traditionally regarded as populists. First, Putin is wary of social activism: he rarely calls the people to act in support of his policies; on the contrary, he seems to capitalise on the well-documented low levels of political activism of Russians[14]. Laruelle calls Putin's attitude "passive patriotism", that is, "passive support for the regime and the marginalisation of contesting forces – but not an active one"[15]. In this respect, he is very different from right-wing populists such as Le Pen, Orbán, and Trump who "seek to stir or provoke their supporters to political involvement"[16]. And he is certainly different from Turkey's Erdoğan: Turkey's ruling party (the Justice and Development Party, or AKP) and his leader rely heavily on public manifestations of consent. Especially after the 15 July coup attempt in 2016, the "will of the people" (*milli irade*) became an ever-present theme in the party's narrative[17] and the president often called the people to take to the streets – not only symbolically: when I was living in Ankara, I personally

---

[14] Youth groups such as Nashi ("Our" in Russian) may be regarded as an exception. After the 2011-12 anti-government protests, the Kremlin made an effort to create an army of politically active youths, creating groups like Nashi. However, these groups are not grassroots and rest on shaky foundations. The political scientist Yekaterina Schulmann believes that "they'll continue to exist as long as they are given official attention. When they don't get any, these groups vanish". M. Tsnompilantze, "Generation Putin: Smug, Patriotic and Rebellious", *The Moscow Time*, 30 April 2018.

[15] M. Laruelle, *Putin's Regime and the Ideological Market: A Difficult Balancing Game*, Carnegie Endowment for International Peace, 2017, p. 5.

[16] M.S. Fish (2017), p. 67.

[17] See I. Toygür, "Turkey's AKP: Nationalism, Populism and Beyond" in this volume.

received text messages from the government with requests to manifest and defend "democracy" on a couple of occasions.

Another feature that tells Putin apart from many classical populist leaders is that, while he definitely can be called a charismatic leader, he manages to "eschew the trappings of a personality cult [...] and prefers to legitimate his authority in rational-legal rather than charismatic terms"[18]. Photos of Putin riding a horse or hunting and cultivating a macho image may make the international headlines, but this is not comparable to the cult of personality of some Soviet or current leaders as Azerbaijan's Ilham Aliyev. Again, the comparison with Turkey is striking: it is very common to see gigantic pictures of Erdoğan on Turkish streets, even beyond the electoral period, to the extent that one can legitimately wonder whether Erdoğan is striving to rival with the cult of Mustafa Kemal Atatürk, whose image is ubiquitous in public spaces and private homes alike. Giant banners portraying Putin are not commonly seen in Russian cities, and the indeed prosperous business of Putin's mugs is, in my opinion, something that is designed for international rather than domestic consumers.

Most importantly, despite Russians' distrust of political elites, Putin has made little efforts to alter the composition of the elites in power. The new government following the March 2018 election saw no big changes in the key positions; even the unpopular Dmitry Medvedev remained in charge as Prime Minister. Change, however, is becoming a necessity. Corruption and painful social reforms are increasingly feeding into populist anti-elitist narratives and are already spurring massive protests[19]. Anti-elitism is a key, if not the most relevant, component of the political discourse of Alexey Navalny, lawyer, activist, and Putin's fierce political opponent. Navalny – who, especially in Western eyes, came to embody the opposition to Putin – has been defined a "right-wing populist" who is the "Scourge of Russia's

---

[18] M.S. Fish (2017), p. 71.
[19] The chief example is that opposition to the proposal of raising the retirement age.

elite". A vocal critic of the corruption that pervades the ruling elites, Navalny believes that Putin "usurped power" and that the imperative of his opponent is to "return power to the people"[20]. The Kremlin is aware of this risk and has consulted the Expert Institute of Social Studies (EISS) think-tank on how to counter a populist upsurge, which may hit the country by the time of the next presidential election in 2024, according to the analysts[21].

In sum, as for the domestic dimension of populism, Putin may adopt some populist themes to boost his popularity; when it comes to his actual governing style, though, he is a deeply conservative and pro-establishment leader, who seems more preoccupied with countering the threatening success of the populist camp rather than leading it.

"Us vs Them": The External Dimension and Nationalism

The external dimension of populism looks for external enemies to be accused of threatening the country, and against which a country's population and its leaders cement their sense of group identity. The search for external enemies is a widely acknowledged feature of populism. Böttcher and Wruuck claim that "it is in the self-interest of populist parties to fuel debates that focus on security/external threats and 'cultural topics', including issues that are often symbolic and emotionally charged"[22]. Schmitter states that "populisms use foreigners and foreign powers as scapegoats for their own failings and weaken external linkages necessary for national welfare and security"[23]. In other

[20] D. Sandford, "Alexei Navalny: Scourge of Russia's elite", *BBC News*, 6 march 2012.

[21] E. Pudovkin, "Vladimir Putin, a man of the people: How the Kremlin is preparing for a populist wave", New Eastern Europe, 7 May 2018.

[22] B. Böttcher and P. Wruuck, *Who is afraid of populists?*, EU Monitor European integration, Deutsche Bank Research, 2017.

[23] P.C. Schmitter (2006). "A balance sheet of the vices and virtues of 'populisms'" European University Institute, papers, April 2006.

words, there is an externalisation of the "elites", which, in some cases, are identified with the wealthy and powerful states making up the category of the "West".

It is mainly in the external dimension that populism appears to meet with nationalism in Russia. Similar to the issue of populism, the question on whether Putin's government is nationalist divides researchers. A majority of experts seem to agree that Putin's nationalism is functional to the achievement of some objectives rather than being a "genuine" component of his government. Laruelle questions the assumption that Russia's foreign policy is "nationalist," commonly used to explain the Ukrainian crisis of 2014: Russia may indeed use a "nationalist post hoc explanation but does not advance a nationalist agenda"[24]. Putin also wants to prevent nationalist movements from gaining excessive power and strives to keep them under control. In a country where roughly 20% of the population does not identify as ethnically Russian, ethnonationalism is particularly risky for it can become a "mobilising slogan against the regime for some ethnically Russian grassroots movements"[25].

However, many experts believe that Putin's government – although it cannot be called nationalist proper – has at times used nationalism to pursue concrete objectives. The use of some of these nationalist themes is of interest in the framework of this study because it mingles with the external dimension of populism. In what follows, I analyse three themes in Kremlin's political discourse, where I believe the search for a political antagonist meets attempts at shaping national identity and restoring Russia's status on the international arena: the defence of compatriots, Western Russophobia, and the defence of conservative values. Each of these topics would deserve a much more in-depth analysis, which unfortunately is not possible to carry out within the scope of this chapter. Yet I aim to point to these

---

[24] M. Laruelle, "Russia as a 'Divided Nation', from Compatriots to Crimea: A Contribution to the Discussion on Nationalism and Foreign Policy", *Problems of Post-Communism*, vol. 62, no. 2, 2015, pp. 88-97, cit. p. 96.
[25] M. Laruelle (2017).

three themes as the crossroads where populism and nationalism meet in Russia, hoping to spur future research on the issue.

Defence of compatriots

The defence of "compatriots" (Russians abroad) is often cited as evidence of Putin's nationalist-populist turn, especially in light of the annexation of Crimea in March 2014. The Kremlin's use of uncommon nationalist rhetoric boosted Putin's popularity: Putin presented himself as the defender of Russians abroad and, at the same time, of Russia's national interests[26]. The Russian diaspora comprises between 25 and 30 million people, being the world's second largest diaspora after the Chinese[27]. In 1992, Boris Yeltsin and Andrei Kozyrev introduced the term 'compatriots abroad' into the political discourse. The term refers to ethnic Russians who live outside Russia's borders but also individuals that are not ethnically or legally Russian, but feel that they have historical, cultural, and language ties with Russia, and want to nurture this relationship regardless of their actual citizenship[28]. Putin stresses the importance of self-perception when defining "compatriots":

> In Ukraine, as you may have seen, at threat were our 'compatriots', Russian people and people of other nationalities, their language, history, culture and legal rights, guaranteed, by the way, by European conventions. When I speak of Russians and Russian-speaking citizens I am referring to 'those people who consider themselves part of the broad Russian community, they may not necessarily be ethnic Russians, but they consider themselves Russian people[29].

---

[26] P. Kolstø, " Crimea vs. Donbas: How Putin Won Russian Nationalist Support- and Lost it Again", *Slavic Review*, vol. 75, no. 3, 2016, pp. 702-25.
[27] M. Suslov, "'Russian World': Russia's Policy towards its Diaspora", IFRI Notes 103, July 2017, p. 5.
[28] President of Russia, Amendments to the law on state policy toward compatriots living abroad, 24 July 2010, http://en.kremlin.ru/events/president/news/8429
[29] V. Putin, Conference of Russian ambassadors and permanent representatives,

Therefore, this broad definition of compatriots speaks to different – and, at times, competing – versions of nationalism, encompassing ethnonationalism, references to the imperial past or Soviet identity, or civic or legal definitions (people with a Russian passport)[30].

Over the last decade, there has been an attempt to engage compatriots through Kremlin-backed organisations that implemented soft power policies with varying degrees of success. While engaging with minorities abroad is a legitimate policy of many homeland states, experts agree that there has been an increasing politicisation of Russian and Russian-speaking minorities[31]. The 2008 war with Georgia was Russia's first usage of the need to defend compatriots as a justification for military action[32]. With the annexation of Crimea, the protection of compatriots became an essential element in the process of furthering external actors. Indeed, Putin defined the ousting of the former Ukrainian President Viktor Yanukovych as a "coup" perpetrated by "[Ukrainian] Nationalists, neo-Nazis, Russophobes and anti-Semites"[33]. But not only has the Kremlin upheld its moral responsibility to defend the Russian "nation abroad" from the "Ukrainian threat", but it also employed an anti-elitist discourse against the West when defending Russia's interests. In the words of Putin:

> We keep hearing from the United States and Western Europe
> that Kosovo is some special case. (…) This is not even double

1 July 2014, http://en.kremlin.ru/events/president/news/46131 (accessed on January 26 2016)

[30] M. Laruelle (2015), p. 88.

[31] M. Suslov (2017); E. Tafuro, "Fatal attraction? Russia's soft power in its neighbourhood", FRIDE Policy Brief no.18, May 2014; M. Nozhenko, Motherland Is Calling You! Motives Behind And Prospects For The New Russian Policy On Compatriots Abroad, St Petersburg European University.

[32] See *The Georgia War, Ten Years On*, ISPI Dossier, August 2018.

[33] "Vladimir Putin addressed State Duma deputies, Federation Council members, heads of Russian regions and civil society representatives in the Kremlin", The Ministry of Foreign Affairs of the Russian Federation, 18 March 2014.

standards; this is amazing, primitive, blunt cynicism. One should not try so crudely to make everything suit their interests, calling the same thing white today and black tomorrow[34].

Therefore, the Kremlin has used a variety of arguments to justify the annexation of Crimea – from denouncing the West's double standards in Kosovo and Iraq to NATO's eastward expansion, to the self-determination rights of Crimeans. The latter argument claims that Crimeans chose to leave Ukraine and join Russia through a referendum in March 2014, which is largely regarded by the EU and Ukraine as unfair and rigged. The argument, however, took hold and was used by many European popu-lists who support Russia's annexation of Crimea. For instance, Matteo Salvini declared in an interview to the Washington Post: "There was a referendum, and 90% of the people voted for the return of Crimea to the Russian Federation […]. Compare it to the fake revolution in Ukraine, which was a pseudo-revo-lution funded by foreign powers – similar to the Arab Spring revolutions […]. There are some historically Russian zones with Russian culture and traditions which legitimately belong to the Russian Federation"[35]. The criticism and furthering of some Western governments increased with the stepping up of the punitive measures against Russia, resulting in the narrative of Russophobia analysed in the following section.

Western Russophobia

Russia has been the target of international political and econom-ic sanctions for several years now. This appears to have driven the increase in the use of the term "Russophobia" – a strong and often irrational hatred for Russia, or the former Soviet Union, especially its political system[36] – in the media and political dis-

---

[34] Ibid.

[35] L. Weymouth, "Italy has done a lot - maybe too much", *Washington Post*, 19 July 2018.

[36] https://www.collinsdictionary.com/dictionary/english/russophobia

course. A 2018 study by the Atlantic Council's Digital Forensic Research Lab uncovered a sharp increase in the use of the terms "Russophobia" and "anti-Russia hysteria" by the Russian Foreign Ministry and by Kremlin-controlled media outlets RT and Sputnik after 2014[37]. These terms are used to frame the international criticism for Russia's political system or recent actions. For instance, following a 2013 European Parliament's resolution containing recommendations to Russia in the field of human rights, the Ministry of Foreign Affairs released a statement: "We observed a truly Russophobe nature in the paragraphs on Russia. Anti-Russian innuendoes of the European Parliament are not new or a rare thing. However, this time the anti-Russian fervour goes beyond all conceivable bounds"[38].

This is not to say that Russophobia is an entirely made-up phenomenon. Stephen F. Cohen, professor emeritus at NYU and Princeton, deplores strikingly Russophobic statements by high-ranking US officials. For instance, he quotes the Director of National Intelligence James Clapper, who said on NBC national television: "the Russians, who typically, are almost genetically driven to co-opt, penetrate, gain favour", while the late Senator John McCain used to characterise Russia as "a gas station masquerading as a country"[39]. In 2009, the prominent US-based Russian scholar Andrei Tsygankov wrote an entire book full with examples of Russophobic comments among the US media and political establishment[40]. Such comments by top officials and by influential political figures reflect a more general climate of distrust among the US population: a poll by Gallup

---

[37] B. Nimmo, "#PutinAtWar: How Russia Weaponized 'Russophobia'", Digital Forensic Research Lab, 2018.

[38] "Answer by the Director of the Information and Press Department of the Russian Ministry of Foreign Affairs, Alexey Bikantov, to the question from RIA Novosti regarding the adoption of a resolution summarising the implementation of the common foreign and security policy in the EU in 2012 by the European Parliament on 24 October 2013", The Ministry of Foreign Affairs of the Russian Federation, 30 October 2013.

[39] S.F. Cohen, "Russophobia in the New Cold War", *The Nation*, 4 April 2018.

[40] A.P. Tsygankov, *Russophobia*, New York, Palgrave Macmillan, 2009.

(March 2018) shows that 72% of American citizens dislike Russia and consider it a significant threat[41].

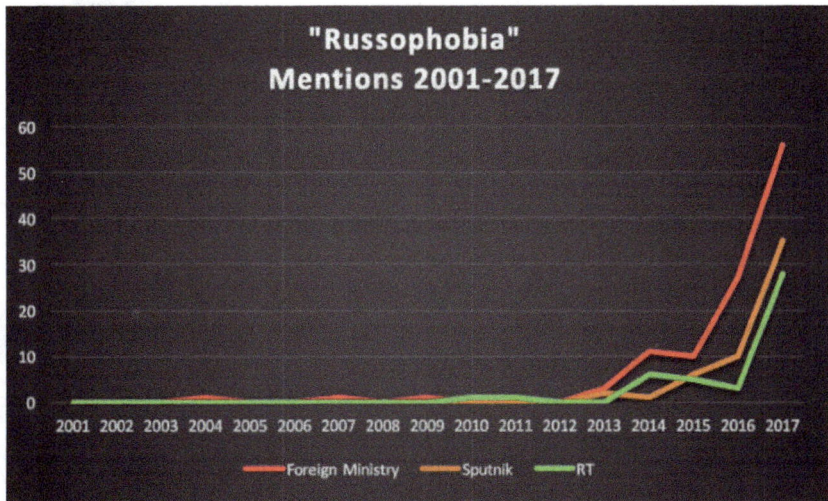

Entries for Sputnik before 2014 refer to its predecessor, Voice of Russia

Source: DFRLab, based on the websites of the Russian Foreign Ministry, Sputnik, and RT

Despite objective evidence of Russophobic attitude, especially in the US, the increase in references to Russophobia seems instrumentalised by the Kremlin to blame the Western elites for the current crisis and its consequences, while boosting national pride among Russians by presenting Russia as a victim of the West. Indeed, "Russophobia" barely featured in Russian official statements before 2014 – only six times from 2001 to the end of 2013 on the English-language version of the Foreign Ministry's website, mainly in connection with the "Magnitsky Act"[42]. In

---

[41] M. Brenan, "Americans, Particularly Democrats, Dislike Russia", Gallup, 5 March 2018.
[42] B. Nimmo (2018).

2017, Putin himself discussed the issue of Russophobia, directly linking it to the Western discomfort with Russia's struggle for
its national interests: "In my opinion, [Russophobia] is because
a multipolar world is being confirmed and monopolists do not
like this. This is happening largely thanks to Russia's struggle for
its interests and, I want to emphasise, for its lawful interests"[43].

Several statements by European populists echoed the
Russophobia argument. France's Marine Le Pen claimed that
Russia is being unfairly "demonised" and that "the campaign
against the Russian political administration has been cooked
up at the highest levels of EU leadership, with the implicit support of the US"[44]. Geert Wilders, the leader of PVV – a Dutch
nationalist and right-wing populist party – claimed that he
wanted to fight against the "hysterical Russophobia that reigns
here", adding that Putin is an ally in the fight against terrorism
and mass immigration from Africa[45].

Blaming the tense state of relations between Russia and the
West on Russophobia is an oversimplification. It is part of the
populist strategy to blame failures on the enemy and to keep
the political space divided: "under Putin's tenure, the West has
become the main foe, once again. Russia [is] turning world politics into a bipolar affair: Russia and its partners against the
US"[46]. The strategy seems to be working, as two out of three
Russians say that their country has enemies – the US being
the biggest adversary[47]. In this regard, it seems that the current
Russophobia in the US and anti-Americanism in Russia are two
sides of the same coin.

[43] Putin explains two reasons behind Western Russophobia, Russia insight, *YouTube*, published on 6 June 2017 https://www.youtube.com/watch?v=Zdu6pgOz-Tw
[44] Le Pen on Ukraine crisis: US pursuing own interests, not those of EU, original article in German: http://www.spiegel.de/politik/ausland/frankreich-le-pen-warnt-merkel-vor-explosion-der-eu-a-972726.html
[45] J. Pieters, "Wilders Defends Russia, Speaks Out Against 'Russophobia'", *nl-times*, 22 November 2017.
[46] P. Casula, "Populism in Power: Lessons from Russia for the future of European populism", Dahrendorf Forum, 2 November 2017.
[47] "Russia's Biggest Enemy Is U.S. – Poll", *The Moscow Times*, 10 January 2018.

Conservatism

The Kremlin's conservative narrative is a prominent instance of the process of combining the construction of Russia's national identity with the identification of external opponents or even enemies. In the words of Robinson and Milne, conservatism marks the start of official populism because the idea of "state-civilisation" based on traditional conservative values creates a "populist logic of equivalence to discredit both 'Western' ideologies of reform and revolution, and unofficial nationalist conceptions of Russianness"[48]. The anti-Western component is particularly strong, and it criticises what Russia perceives as the West's normative imperialism. Indeed, over the last years, Putin's government has been increasingly depicting Russia as an "alternative geopolitical pole with an anti-liberal social outlook [...] in opposition to the West"[49]. Stressing Russia's traditional values and differences from Western countries is a key component of this narrative. In the 2013 presidential address to the Russian Federal Assembly, Putin outlined his conservative vision and presented the EU and the West more generally as decadent places where traditions and values are "eroding", accepting "without question the equality of good and evil"[50]. Despite the divorce from his wife[51], Putin is ready to depict himself as a keen supporter of the traditional family, threatened by liberal elites:

> This destruction of traditional values from above not only leads to negative consequences for society but is also essentially anti-democratic, since it is carried out on the basis of abstract, speculative ideas, contrary to the will of the majority, which does not accept the changes occurring or the proposed revision of values. We know that there are more and more people in the world who support our position on defending traditional values that

---

[48] N. Robinson and S. Milne (2017), p. 421

[49] E. Tafuro (2014), p. 2.

[50] V. Putin, "Presidential Address to the Federal Assembly", President of Russia, 12 December 2013.

[51] See M. Lipman, "The Putin Divorce: What Russia's Rulers Hide", *The New Yorker*, 8 June 2013.

have made up the spiritual and moral foundation of civilisation in every nation for thousands of years: the values of traditional families, real human life, including religious life, not just material existence but also spirituality, the values of humanism and global diversity[52].

At the same time, Putin attacked the US' and EU's democracy promotion activities as attempts to destabilise order and change the culture of other states. Putin declared that "Peoples and countries are raising their voices in favour of self-determination and civilisational and cultural identity, which conflicts with the attempts by certain countries to maintain their domination in the military sphere, in politics, finance, economy and in ideology"[53].

In a diverse mosaic of ethnicities and confessions such as Russia, conservatism is a less problematic way to cement national identity than ethnonationalism or religion. It is a loose narrative, one that can be moulded to include as many people as possible or to fit practical political action according to the circumstances. Laruelle calls it an "ideological market" where the Kremlin offers an "explicit but blurry narrative of conservatism"[54]. It includes anti-Westernism, anti-liberalism, and the promotion of conservative moral values, offering at the same time an implicit ideological diversity in which as many people as possible can find their place. Apart from being loose, this narrative is also conservative in political terms: being grounded in cultural/moral values, it does not question the organisation of the state in Russia or elsewhere, so it champions the status quo, failing to offer an alternative. The only "positive" things that this narrative prescribes in policy terms is the "preservation of Russian culture and its increased celebration and use in education, and the persecution of those who are not part of Putin's community of values"[55].

---

[52] V. Putin (2013).

[53] Ibid.

[54] M. Laruelle (2017), p. 2.

[55] N. Robinson and S. Milne (2017), p. 423.

But how conservative Russian society really is? Conservative attitudes indeed are on the rise: a poll on sexual and reproductive behaviour conducted in December 2017 by the Levada Centre shows a steep increase in conservative views regarding abortion, gay marriage and adultery across Russian society compared to two similar polls from 1998 and 2008[56]. Yet the country has one of the world's highest divorce and abortion rates; when it comes to issues such as birth rate or premarital sex, Russia is not dissimilar from Western European societies[57]. Hence, the image of a rapidly expanding conservatism in Russia's society should not be overestimated[58]. Nevertheless, this narrative has been successful both at the domestic and international level. As Ferrari argues, "Within the country, the stress on conservatism produced a largely shared platform of cultural and moral values that only a minority of Russian citizens seem to refuse [...]. In foreign policy, it has allowed Russia to find a common language with many non-Western countries and even with representatives of conservatism in Europe and the United States"[59].

However, it is noteworthy that many of those who back Russia's conservative stances and see the country as a model are members of illiberal, far-right and populist groups challenging Western liberal democracies from within[60]. Matthew Heimbach – the founder of the Traditionalist Worker Party, a White-Power American group fighting "anti-Christian degeneracy" – claimed that Russia is the movement's biggest inspiration, Putin being the "leader of the free world"[61]. According to Vegas Tenold, a

[56] https://www.levada.ru/2018/01/11/17389/

[57] M. Lipman, "The Battle Over Russia's Anti-Gay Law", *The New Yorker*, 10 August 2013.

[58] A. Ferrari, "Russia. A Conservative Society?", in Idem (ed.), *Russia 2018 Predictable Elections, Uncertain Future*, Milano, Ledizioni-ISPI, 2018, p. 41.

[59] Ibid., p. 51.

[60] Support from far-right groups is at odds with another narrative that describes Russia as an anti-imperialist power – fighting fascism in Ukraine or countering US unilateralism – which is popular among left-wing groups and politicians around the world.

[61] A. Feuer and A. Higgins, "Extremists Turn to a Leader to Protect Western

journalist reporting on neo-Nazi movements, not only are all
the Nazis and nationalists in America vying for the affection of
Russia, but Russia has become the beacon of white nationalism
in the world[62]. In the EU, populist and xenophobic politicians
do not hide their admiration for Putin. For instance, Le Pen
called Putin "a true patriot and defender of European values"[63],
allegedly buying into the narrative of some members of Russia's
political elite, such as Dmitry Rogozin, who define "Russia as
the 'true Europe', continuing Europe's XIX century traditions
of geopolitical spheres of influence and social conservatism"[64].
Although admiration for Putin and support for his conservative outlook do not come exclusively from the far-right
and populists, Russia's "bad influence" on EU's politics worries liberal elites. While the Kremlin's alleged direct financial
support to far-right groups is difficult to trace[65], Moscow is
accused of setting a "bad example" not only for other post-Soviet countries, but also for Eurosceptic governments of several
Eastern European countries, and beyond. A 2016 Report by a
US-based human rights NGO denounces the proliferation of
"Russian-style [...] laws suppressing freedom of assembly and
expression", which are "legitimised by reference to protection
of children, anti-LGBT propaganda laws and other forms of

Values: Vladimir Putin", *The New Times*, 3 December 2016.
[62] L. Beckett, "My six years covering neo-Nazis: 'They're all vying for the affec-
tions of Russia", *The Guardian*, 17 February 2018.
[63] A. Polyakova, "Strange Bedfellows: Putin and Europe's Far Right", *World
Affairs*, vol. 177, no. 3, September/October 2014, pp. 36-40.
[64] J. Lough et al., *Russian Influence Abroad: Non-state Actors and Propaganda*, Russia
and Eurasia Programme Meeting Summary, Chatham House, 2014, p. 2.
[65] In Italy, two populist parties – the Five-Star movement and the League – are
often referred to as "the Kremlin Trojan Horses". However, the nature of their
links to Russia is murky. A 2017 Report claims that while these parties and their
leaders receive media support, primarily in the form of visibility in Kremlin-
backed international media such as Sputnik, there is no publicly available evidence that Moscow has provided them with overt or covert financial support.
See: L.S. Germani and J. Iacoboni, "Italy: Is The Turn To Russia Reversible?",
in A. Polyakova et al., *Kremlin's Trojan Horses*, Atlantic Council Eurasia Centre,
2017, p. 12.

'traditional values'"[66]. It is therefore understandable why liberal EU elites look at Russia's conservatism as probably the most threatening aspect among Russia's nationalist-populist narratives, having dangerous spillovers not only for Russia but for EU politics as well.

Conclusions

In this chapter, I tackled the complex issue of the intersection between populism and nationalism in Russia. I argue that, if both the internal and external dimensions of populism are taken into account, it is not straightforward to call Putin or his government "populist". However, it appears that, especially since 2014, the Kremlin has been increasingly recurring to populist themes, mixing them with nationalist ones. While more research is needed to explore the nexus between the external dimension of populism and nationalism in Russia, I suggest that this nexus reveals itself especially in three of the Kremlin's narratives: the defence of compatriots, Western Russophobia, and the defence of conservative values. The latter narrative is particularly attractive among Western populist leaders. In the EU, many populist leaders admire Russia and share a common set of priorities on restricting immigration, countering the EU and NATO expansion, fighting Islamic radicalism, and resist cultural liberalism and secularisation.

Russia's "bad example" is sometimes coupled with allegations of the Kremlin's financial and/or logistical support to some of the EU's populist and far-right groups. While these allegations certainly need to be investigated thoroughly and, when backed with evidence, dealt with appropriately, overestimating the role of Russia in instigating populism in the EU is a mistake. There is no question about Russia's effort in countering Western liberal narratives and shaping global public opinion,

---

[66] M. Hooper, *Russia's Bad Example*, Free Russia Foundation, Human Rights First, February 2016, p. 7.

also through Kremlin-funded media outlets. However, the link between Russia and the rise of populism in Europe and elsewhere is far less clear. While populist and far-right leaders may admire Putin, he did not create them and is not the reason they gain popular support[67]. In fact, people who support these groups do not necessarily have a good opinion on Russia. To the contrary: a 2017 Pew survey showed that unfavourable attitudes toward Russia and its President are widespread in the EU, even in countries where Russia-friendly populist and far-right parties are strong. For instance, half of the Hungarians hold an unfavourable opinion on Russia, and almost 60% do not trust Putin's Russia on the international stage. In Italy – often considered as one of Russia's closest friends in the EU – the figures are 54% and 64%, respectively[68].

The reasons why voters turn to populist parties are mainly economy- and identity-related. Some of their concerns are inflated by inaccurate and noxious media and social media campaigns; others – such as the dismantling of welfare state due to the EU's austerity measures – are legitimate concerns that should be addressed. Governments at all levels need to make an effort to tackle fake news and external interferences, but also to help citizens navigate the variety of sources available and read them critically. At the same time, they need to invest in making the EU model – a mix of market economy and redistribution through welfare – attractive again.

---

[67] O. Oliker (2017), p. 19. For a comprehensive review on the highly-debated issue of whether Russia is engaging in "autocracy promotion", see K. Yakouchyk, "Beyond Autocracy Promotion: A Review", *Political Studies Review*, 2018, doi: 10.1177/1478929918774976.

[68] M. Vice, "Publics Worldwide Unfavorable Toward Putin", Russia, Pew Research Centre, 16 August 2017.

7. "Democraduras"?
Venezuela and National-Populism in Latin America

Carlos de la Torre, Federico Finchelstein

How does a populist leader become a dictator? How is populism different from previous forms of authoritarian nationalism? Those are the questions Venezuelans are now grappling with. These queries should serve as a warning to the United States and other countries with national populists in power like Hungary, Poland, and Turkey. Venezuelan President Nicolás Maduro turned away from the legacy of his mentor and predecessor, Hugo Chávez, eschewing authoritarian democracy for straight-up autocracy. The Freedom House, for example, considered Venezuela not free for the first time in 2016.

Maduro is not the first Latin American populist who became a tyrant. In 1992 Alberto Fujimori in Peru gave a self-coup and closed Congress. He was a dictator for about seven months when a new Congress was elected. Then, in 1993, a new Constitution was approved by referendum and Fujimori was reelected with 64% of the votes in free elections in 1995[1]. His autocratic regime finally collapsed in 2000, and democracy was reinstated under the presidency of Valentín Paniagua.

---

[1] M. Tanaka, "Peru 1980-2000: Chronicle of a Death Foretold? Determinism, Political Decisions, and Open Outcomes" in F.Hagopian and S.P. Mainwaring (eds.), *The Third Way of Democratization in Latin America. Advances and Setbacks*, Cambridge, Cambridge University Press, 2005, p. 263.

After the third wave of democratisation, coups often failed in Latin America. This was a novelty because from the 1930s to the 1970s, the cycle populism-dictatorship marked the history of Argentina, Brazil, Ecuador, Panama, Peru, and Bolivia. When the international community recognised the vote as the only legitimate tool to elect and remove presidents it forced autocrats like Maduro to use elections. Yet, from the 16 elections between 1999 and 2012 won by Hugo Chávez and certified by the OAS and other supranational organisations as clean, the legitimacy of the elections of May 2018 in Venezuela was not recognised.

Trump's Reaction

The American right and the populist Trump administration, whose disregard for legality and basic democratic procedures have more in common with Maduro's cavalier disregard for basic democratic features than they'd ever admit, sharply criticised Venezuela's regime. In July 2017, President Trump, the American caudillo, described Maduro as a "bad leader" and an aspiring "dictator". By August, Trump had threatened war against Venezuela, and the White House explicitly said Maduro's government was a dictatorship.

Some have even wondered if Trump was trying to encourage a coup. It wouldn't be the first time an American administration did so. After all, many figures in the opposition, as well as the United States, supported a failed anti-Chávez coup in 2002. And perhaps the Trump administration would like to see a more successful effort to unseat Maduro. But ultimately the American government is betting on domestic polarisation to do the work of removing Maduro.

In 2017, Vice President Pence provided an ideological framework for Trump's comments by saying that "The birthright of the Venezuelan people has always been and will always be libertad". The Trump's administration's notion of freedom, however, is not necessarily tied to a defense of constitutional democracy, given that the White House is populated by leaders who find good people among neo-Nazis and KKK demonstrators, who embolden racist views by practicing religious discrimination and racial profiling of immigrants, and who came to power as the result of the most racist campaign in recent history. Rather, "freedom" for Trumpism is the ability to decide in the name of the people what is best for the president. This is populism in a nutshell, and helps us better understand its connection to authoritarianism and nationalism.

Populism and Nationalism

Populists promised to return power to the people, and to put the interests of their nations first. Their appeal to the people and nation however tends to differ in the north and in the global south, and between right and left[2]. Whereas rightwing populists like the Trumps or the Le Pens use ethnicity, race, religion, and culture to define the nation and the people, excluding the non-white and formerly colonial populations from their restrictive view of the heartland, leftwing populists in the global south and the north use socioeconomic constructs to define the people and its enemies. For the left, the people are those excluded sectors of the population that recognise the leader, and those who don't are presented as the anti-people. For the populist right, the enemies are also ethnically different. Trump for example imagined the American people as white, Christian, and law-abiding using the images of the Mexican, the Muslim terrorist, and the African American militant to mark the key distinctions between the people and its enemies. Chávez and other leftwing populists in Southern Europe or Latin America constructed the struggle as one between the people and the oligarchy that appropriated political and economic power to serve

---

[2] D. Filc "Latin American Inclusive and European Exclusionary Populism: Colonialism and an Explanation", *Journal of Political Ideologies*, vol. 20, no. 3, 2015, pp. 263-83.

the interests of imperialist powers. Whereas ethnic and cultural notions of the nation and the people are inherently exclusionary, socioeconomic constructs could be inclusionary for those that decide to join the camp of the leader of the people.

Yet despite its inclusionary policies, when in power populists used national and populist tropes to transform rivals into enemies, while thinking their leader is the incarnation of the people and the nation. The two most paradigmatic populist experiences, Peronism and Chavism, showed the ambiguities between inclusion and autocracy. Perón in the 1940s and the 1950s and again in the 1970s, and Chavez at the turn of the XXI century led the most dramatic processes of political, socioeconomic, and cultural inclusion. Voter turnout under Peronism dramatically surged from 18% of the population in 1946 to 50% in 1955. Peron's administration expanded the franchise by giving women the right to vote in 1951. In that election, seven women became senators, and 24 women were elected to Congress. Perón's government redistributed wealth and increased the share of wages as a share of GDP from 37% in 1946 to 47% in 1955. Workers received other material benefits such as access to social and medical services, and paid vacations[3]. Chávez's administration equated the interests of the nation with the interests of ordinary people, putting the state in charge of economic development. Oil production was nationalised in 2001, and steel, telecommunications, and electric industries followed suit. His government reversed neoliberalism while incrementing its reliance on oil exports to 96%. Venezuela reaped huge benefits from the commodity boom of the 2000s, which sent oil prices to record levels. As a result of enhanced revenues, public investment and social spending skyrocketed, and poverty rates – and to a lesser extent inequality – fell while the prices of oil remained high. World Bank figures indicate that the poverty rate in Venezuela fell from 55.4% of the population

---

[3] C. de la Torre, "Populism and Nationalism in Latin America", *Javnost-The Public*, vol. 24, no. 4, 2017, pp. 376-77.

in 2002 to 28.5% in 2009. But the falling oil prices led to an increase of poverty in Venezuela. According to the Economic Commission for Latin America, poverty rates jumped from 24% in 2012 to 32% in 2013. Another study concluded that 75% of Venezuelans were poor according to their income levels in 2015[4].

Perón and Chávez controlled all institutions of the state, sparring with the media and with autonomous social movements and other civil society organisations. These populist leaders constructed politics as confrontations against enemies that on the discursive level needed to be destroyed. Perón argued that when political adversaries became "enemies of the nation" they were no longer "gentlemen that one should fight fairly but snakes that one can kill in any way"[5]. Similarly, Chávez did not face political rivals, but the oligarchy defined as "those self-serving elites who work against the homeland"[6]. Like Perón he did not murder his opponents, but he used an aggressive language to portray them as enemies of the people and the nation. Populists demonise their enemies, even rendering them politically illegitimate but they also need them to participate and be defeated in more or less open elections.

The paradoxes between authoritarianism and inclusion are illustrated in populist educational policies. At the same time that these regimes gave access to previously marginalised groups, their educational policies aimed to create Peronist or Bolivarian national subjects. As in fascism, but now coupled with democratic procedures, the leader, the nation and the people were equated into one single entity. In both fascist dictatorship and populist democracy, the leader is constructed as the representative but also the personification of an entire people, nation and even history. Under both regimes, the leader decides in the

---

[4] Ibid, p. 379.

[5] F. Finchelstein, *The Ideological Origins of the Dirty War*, Oxford, Oxford University Press, 2014, p. 86.

[6] P. Zuquete, "The Missionary Politics of Hugo Chavez", *Latin American Politics and Society*, vol. 50, no. 1, 2008, p. 105.

name of a political trinity that he embodies[7]. Party, leader, and State were unified. In a speech delivered in 1953, Perón defined himself as the first indoctrinator of the nation who "delegates to the Argentinean teachers and professors the responsibility of inculcating [the Peronist doctrine] in the children and youth of the New Argentina"[8]. Similarly, article 107 of the 1999 Constitution stated that the principles of Bolivarian ideology had to be taught in all schools in Venezuela.

Textbooks were Peronised in Argentina and Bolivarianised in Venezuela. Eva Perón's autobiography became mandatory reading at all levels of education, and children learned to read and write their first words with sentences such as Evita loves me or Perón loves children. The curriculum of Bolivarian schools taught about Bolívar's legacy and the struggles of the founding fathers for sovereignty, national independence, and social justice. Chávez was not mentioned directly, yet as sociologist Manuel Anselmi argues in his study of Bolivarian schools, "there is a tacit hope that once children grow, they will transfer their respect and devotion for the symbols and icons of classical Bolivarianism to [Chávez's] revolutionary Bolivarianism"[9].

Both Perón and Chávez were portrayed as carriers of the unfinished missions of exemplary nationalist figures. Perón declared that 1950 was the year of General San Martín. Like the founding father that led Argentina's struggle for political independence by expelling the Spanish empire, Perón was conquering economic independence by expelling imperialists from Argentina. Chávez was erected into the carrier of Bolívar's project of national and continental liberation. To celebrate the 10th anniversary of his presidency, Chávez visited the tomb of Bolívar and asserted: "Ten years ago, Bolívar –embodied in the

---

[7] F. Finchelstein, *From Fascism to Populism in History*, Oakland, University of California Press, 2017, p. 252.
[8] M. Plotkin, *Mañana es San Perón. A Cultural History of Peron's Argentina*, Wilmington, Scholarly Resources, 2003, p. 100.
[9] M. Anselmi, *Chavez's Children. Ideology, Education, and Society in Latin America.*, Lanham, Lexington Books, 2013, p. 132.

will of the people – came back to life"[10].

Hugo Chávez, Juan and Eva Perón were transformed into mythical and even religious-like figures. Evita asserted that "Perón is a God", while other Peronist professed that "God is Peronist"[11]. She referred to Perón's Argentina as "the promised land" and to Perón as its "savior" and "redeemer". Eva Perón herself was portrayed as a saint: "She was the First Samaritan, the Lady of Hope, and just before her death, she became the Spiritual Leader of the Nation"[12]. State employees were compelled to attend weekly "doctrinal lectures" with topics such as "The Word of Perón". It was mandatory that pictures of Perón adorned lecture halls during the "indoctrination"[13]. Watching propaganda movies about the Peróns and their work was also mandatory.

Chavez's followers elevated him into a saint-like figure with the powers to heal. In 1999 an elderly woman grabbed him by the arm to beg "Chávez, help me, my son has paralysis". A crying young man stopped him outside the door of Caracas Cathedral and yelled: "Chávez help me, I have two sons that are dying of hunger and I do not want to become a delinquent, save me from this inferno"[14].

Between Democracy and Autocracy

When populism first emerged in Argentina in the 1940s most left-leaning intellectuals branded Peronism as fascism. Contrary to this common sense explanation the first major theorist of populism Gino Germani showed its ambiguities

---

[10] C. Lindholm and J.P. Zúquete, *The Struggle for the World*, Stanford, Stanford University Press, 2010, p. 24.

[11] F. Finchelstein (2014), p. 80.

[12] M. Plotkin (2003), p. 159.

[13] F. Finchelstein (2014), p. 81.

[14] A.T. Torres, *La herencia de la tribu. Del mito de la independencia a la revolución bolivariana*, Caracas, Editorial ALFA, 2009, p. 229.

for democratisation[15]. He argued that populism was inclusionary and led to the fundamental democratisation of Argentina
while belonging to the autocratic family. The ambivalences of
populism were later lost in the literature. Marxist scholars like
Carlos Vilas reinterpreted populism as democratising and inclusionary, overlooking its autocratic policies so well analysed
by Germani[16]. Ernesto Laclau wrote perhaps the most sophisticated defense of leftwing populism as the political[17]. His followers are promoting leftwing populism as the only alternative
to pos-democracies, and as the only available strategy to stop
the xenophobic right[18].

Liberal political scientists followed a different interpretation
of the relationship between populism and democratisation.
Forgetting about populist inclusion, and silencing the populist
critique to existing exclusionary institutions populism is presented as the main danger to democracy. Under weak institutions, Levitsky and Loxton argued it is the forerunner of competitive authoritarianism[19]. Whereas some are optimistic about
the resilience of US democratic institutions[20], others are rightly
afraid that Trumpism would lead to unprecedented processes of
democratic erosion[21].

The tale of Venezuela's democracy shows how populism is
both an answer to the crises of disfigured democracies, and its
main danger. Like other populists in Latin America, Chavez's

---

[15] G. Germani, *Authoritarianism, Fascism, and National Populism*, New Brunswick,
Transaction Books, 1978.
[16] C. Vilas, "Estudio preliminar: El populismo o la democratización fundamental de América Latina", in *La democratización fundamental: El populismo en América
Latina*, México, Consejo Nacional para la Cultura y las Artes 1995, pp. 11-118.
[17] E. Laclau, *On Populist Reason*, London and New York, Verso, 2005.
[18] I. Errejón and C. Mouffe, *Construir Pueblo. Hegemonía y radicalización de la democracia*, Madrid, Icaria, 2015.
[19] S. Levitsky and J. Loxton, "Populism and Competitive Authoritarianism in the
Andes", *Democratization*, vol. 20, no. 1, 2013, pp. 107-136.
[20] K. Weyland and R. Madrid, "Liberal democracy, stronger than populism so
far", *The American Interest*, vol. 13, no. 4, 2018, pp. 24-29.
[21] S. Levitsky and D. Ziblat, *How Democracies Die*, New York, Crown Publishing, 2017.

was inclusionary, promised a better democracy, and during most of his term in office there were experiments of democratic innovation. Yet, as in other populisms, its autocratic view of politics as the struggle between friend and enemy, its appropriation of the concept of the nation to cast all critics as peons of US imperialism, and the transformation of a leader into a Messianic figure ultimately led to authoritarianism.

Will all populist regimes face similar fates than as Venezuela's? Not quite. Stronger democratic institutions and a more complex civil society were impediments for a populist rupture in Argentina under the Kirchners. In Greece stronger democratic national and supranational institutions limit what Alexis Tsipras can do in power, and in 2015 Siryza ultimately capitulated to the dictates of the Troika. In Ecuador, Lenín Moreno, Correa's handpicked successor, is dismantling his mentor's autocratic control of all institutions of justice and accountability, and won a referendum in 2018 to finish with Correa's possibility to run again for office. It is also good to remember that populist autocrats are often giants with feet of clay. After Fujimori seemed to have a firm grip of power after the fraudulent elections of 2000, his rightwing autocratic regime collapsed when he broke with his chief of intelligence Vladiviro Motesinos amid scandals of corruption, widespread bribery, abuses of power, and widespread violations of human rights. Populism thrives in polarisation but polarisation also explains its inner tensions and ultimate failures.

Populist Hybrid Regimes

The tensions that define authoritarian populism run through its history, from Argentine Peronism to Chavismo to Trumpism. Populism is, in fact, a form of authoritarianism that distorts and narrows democracy without destroying it. In fact, as Nadia Urbinati argues, populism is a disfigurement of democracy[22].

---

[22] N. Urbinati, *Democracy Disfigured*, Cambridge, Harvard University Press, 2014.

In most populist regimes democracies become illiberal, with populists defining their leader and followers as the entire people and all those who disagree as enemies of the people.

And yet this demonisation of the opposition and the independent press, as well as the executive's increasing colonisation of the other branches of government, are not accompanied by the elimination of these democratic fixtures from the political system. In the history of most populist regimes there was no significant move from rhetorical demonisation to actual persecution. And unlike the fascists (who are their predecessors, their ideological cousins and their eventual allies), populists find in electoral victories a key source of their legitimacy. Populists, in short, do not completely ignore the most basic tenets of democratic constitutions[23].

Historically, Latin American populists polarised their societies, but they did not engage in high levels of repression and political violence. Over the past two decades, Latin American populism married electoral democracy with authoritarian leadership[24]. This was the case of Venezuela under Chávez. Electoral majorities almost always supported his populist regime. But he also severely downplayed the separation of powers and strengthened the army and popular militias, even occasionally engaging in anti-Semitism and demonising the press and more generally dissent. Although Comandante Chávez had once participated in a coup (as Argentine populist leader Juan Perón had done in 1930 and 1943), he was later fully committed to democratic elections while limiting other democratic traditions. Thus, generally Latin American populism embraced the authoritarian forms of democracy that defined it so well.

When Chávez was elected, Venezuela's democracy was undergoing a profound crisis. From the 1950s to the 1970s political scientists considered Venezuela as one of the most successful cases of transition from dictatorship to democracy, and of

---

[23] F. Finchelstein (2017).
[24] C. de la Torre, *Populist Seduction in Latin America*, Athens, Ohio University Press, 2010.

political stability with a well-functioning two-party system. In a region where in the 1970s dictators were the rule rather than the exception, Venezuela was a democracy since 1958. However, its overreliance on oil exports brought crises and instability when prices dropped. Inequality surge in the 1980s and 1990s, and Venezuela's democracy was disfigured with a lack of responsiveness and accountability of its political elites[25]. The two major cartel parties were involved in cases of corruption, followed IMF's receipts regardless of what citizens had voted for, abandoned oil policies based on national sovereignty, and the state used violence to repress protests. The insurgency against the hike in the price of gasoline known as El Caracazo of 1989 ended with at least 400 people killed by the state, and buried whatever legitimacy was left of the two-party system. Chávez won the 1999 election by promising to improve democracy, and to send "the rotten" elites of the parties "to the trash bin of history".[26] Once in power, his government launched a series of experiments of participatory democracy such as the Bolivarian Circles and the Communal Councils. He abandoned neoliberalism, and overhauled his nation's foreign policy with anti-imperialism and the creation of alternative supranational institutions without the US like the Bolivariana Alliance (ALBA).

Unlike Chávez who displaced Venezuela's malfunctioning democracy towards hybridity, Maduro stopped following the most basic democratic procedures altogether. He went against constitutional mandates, dissolved congress, exiled dissenting members of the judiciary, engaged in high levels of repression and ignored the most elementary electoral norms. His regime ceased to be "populist" and became something else: dictatorship. This is what is happening in Venezuela today.

Maduro is reaching this unusual moment in the transformation from populism to dictatorship. He has banned and

---

[25] K.M. Roberts, "Populism, Political Mobilizations, and Crises of Political Representation", in C. de la Torre (ed.), *The Promise and Perils of Populism: Global Perspectives*, Lexington, The University Press of Kentucky, 2015, p. 149.

[26] Hugo Chávez quoted in K.M. Roberts (2015), p. 150.

imprisoned members of the opposition. His government is responsible for the killing of more than a hundred citizens, establishing a constitutional assembly with a dubious single-party vote that has practically voided his country's separation of powers. His regime also occupied congress and declared itself above all other powers. His base of support is the military, and relies on cronyism and corruption to keep a small clique in power – including the relatives of the Chávez and Maduro families[27]. In conditions of widespread shortages of food and medicine, he uses the distribution of food in exchange for votes. Maduro's legitimacy also lies in the consecration of Chavez into a secular saint and of Bolivarianism as a political theology. Maduro buried Chávez in a newly-built pantheon to "symbolise the renaissance of the homeland and the immeasurable life of Eternal Commandant"[28].

Some pundits dismiss the tragedy of Venezuela as typical of Latin America's history of strong men. Recent history shows it is not. Contrary to stereotypes about the region, the current situation in Venezuela is quite uncommon. Latin American countries (including governments on the non-populist left such as Uruguay and Chile) denounced Maduro, and the OAS did not accept as legitimate the May 2018 elections. The new assembly has been equally criticised by intellectuals on the Latin American left, former members of the left-wing social movement Chavismo like Maduro's former Minister of the Interior, Miguel Rodríguez Torres, or the now-exiled attorney general, Luisa Ortega, as well as, in a very timid manner, Pope Francis.

Generally devoid of the racism of North American populists, populists in Latin American history have combined intolerant and absolutist understandings of their exclusive representation of the people as a whole with electoral wins – a history with

---

[27] M. López Maya, *El ocaso del chavismo. Venezuela 2005-2015*, Caracas, Editorial ALFA, 2016.
[28] Quoted in M. González Trejo, *Pueblo y democracia en el populismo venezolano*, unpublished Ph.D. dissertation, Departamento de Ciencia Política y Relaciones Internacionales, Univeridad Autónoma de Madrid, 2017, p. 139.

echoes in Trump's administration as much as the origins of the Maduro regime.

Some Historical Lessons

It is unclear whether European or American forms of right-wing populism, including Trumpism, are equally committed to some basic democratic values. Fascism is always looming above populism, especially in Europe and the United States, where neo-fascist and "alt-right" movements have grown in strength and numbers.

It is odd that, in this sense, Venezuela's dictatorial measures are closer to the United States than to Latin America. In sharp contrast with most Latin American versions of populism, which after re-formulating and leaving behind fascism after 1945 became firmly rooted in formal democracy, North American populism combines racism and discrimination, the demonisation of dissenters and the independent media with what is so far a dubious authoritarian position toward the working of the judicial system, including the investigation on Russian interference in the 2016 election.

Trumpism is authoritarian and populist but not yet dictatorial. And yet, at the present moment, the country where modern liberal democracy was born runs the risk of returning the populist phenomenon to its dictatorial foundations.

This is already happening in Venezuela. The dictatorial detour of the Venezuelan ruling class – from a messianic, corrupt but elected leadership to its present debacle – sends a warning sign to the north rather than the south of the Rio Grande. No democratic Latin American country today has authoritarian presidents like Trump and Maduro. Perhaps the United States could learn something from Latin American history. Its populist neighbours to the south were never as extreme as the present Venezuelan and American strongmen.

The tragedy of Venezuela is explained by the success of Chávez in naming a successor, the unity of the armed forces and most of the Chavista elites behind Maduro, the failures of the opposition in using the electoral and the insurrectionist routes, and so far the inability of the international community to cope with this trend of populist regimes turning into dictatorships. Under Maduro, Venezuelans are suffering from hunger, lack of medicines, the biggest diaspora in the history of the country, high levels of insecurity, and widespread repression.

The US is not Venezuela and it is unlikely that its democratic system will implode under Trump. The same might be said for countries like Italy or Austria with their extreme-right populist coalitions.

In the United States, a plural civil society, and an independent media have been so far the biggest opponent to Trump's autocratic policies[29]. After his inauguration thousand took he streets to protect women's right, and later marched against his "Muslim ban", to defend science, and thousands of high school students demanded gun control. These encouraging acts of resistance have emboldened the Democratic Party. Yet, to please its more reactionary base Republicans continue to surrender their party principles to Trump's authoritarianism. If Trumpist control the Republican Party, and if the Democrats do not take over the House and the Senate in 2018 the prospects for democracy are gloomy indeed.

Trump's brand of racist populism is the biggest threat to an inclusive and plural public sphere[30]. This risk is a global one, and it has happened before with transnational fascism. From Hungary to the Philippines and beyond, the example of Trumpism is encouraging and enabling autocrats to redouble their attacks against constitutional democracy. Moreover, if in the United States the Republican Party continues to move to the extreme and xenophobic right, and if the alt-right and other fascist groups continue to gain strength, the US could possibly become the precursor of a new wave of autocracies.

---

[29] A. Arato and J.L. Cohen, "Civil Society, Populism, and Religion", *Constellations*, vol. 24, 2017, pp. 283-95.
[30] C. de la Torre, "Trumps Populism. Lessons from Latin America", *Postcolonial Studies*, vol. 20, no. 2, 2017, pp. 187-98.

The Authors

Carlos de la Torre is a Professor of Sociology at the University of Kentucky and Emeritus Professor at FLACSO-Ecuador. His latest books are his edited volumes: *Latin American Populism in the Twenty-First Century*, co-edited with Cynthia J. Arnson (2013), *The Promise and Perils of Populism: Global Perspectives* (2015), and *The Routledge Handbook of Global Populism* (2019).

Federico Finchelstein is a Professor of History at the New School for Social Research and Eugene Lang College. He is Director of the Janey Program in Latin American Studies at NSSR. Professor Finchelstein is the author of six books on fascism, populism, Dirty Wars, the Holocaust and Jewish history in Latin America and Europe. His new book is: *From Fascism to Populism in History* (2017). He has been a contributor to major American, European, and Latin American newspapers and media.

Kirk A. Hawkins is a Professor of Political Science at Brigham Young University (Utah, Usa). He is the Director of Team Populism, a cross-regional scholarly network studying populism's causes and consequences. He is the co-editor of *The Ideational Approach to Populism: Concept, Theory, and Analysis* (2019).

Karin Liebhart is a Political Scientist. She is a Fulbright Visiting Associate Professor of Political Science at the University of Minnesota; Senior Lecturer at the University of Vienna. Her Research focus in on Political Communication, Discursive and Visual Representations of Politics, Right-wing Populism and Extremism.

Radoslaw Markowski is a Professor of Political Science, at the Center for the Study of Democracy (Director), University of Social Sciences and Humanities and PI of the Polish National Election Study. Recurring Visiting Professor at CEU, Budapest. He has published in peer reviewed journals. Main books: *Post-communist Party Systems* (Cambridge UP 1999, co-author), *Europeanising Party Politics?* (Manchester UP 2011, co-editor) and *Democratic Audit of Poland* (Peter Lang 2015, co-author). An expert of the Varieties of Democracy (V-Dem), Bertelsmann SGI project and Dahrendorf Forum at the Hertie School of Governance.

Alberto Martinelli is Professor Emeritus of Political Science and Sociology, former Dean of the Faculty of Political Sciences of the University of Milan, President of the International Social Science Council, ISPI Senior Advisor. Chairman of the Aem Foundation, A2A Group. Vice President of Science for Peace, Veronesi Foundation. Member of the Lombard Institute of Sciences and Letters. Editorialist at *Corriere della Sera*. Grand official of the Order of Merit of the Italian Republic; Gold Medal from the city of Milan; Member of the Lombardy Institute of Sciences and Letters. Among his recent publications: *La società europea* (with Alessandro Cavalli) (2015); "Sub-national Nationalism and the Catalan Puzzle", in A. Colombo, P. Magri (eds.), *Big Powers Are Back. What About Europe* (2018).

Eleonora Tafuro Ambrosetti is a Research Fellow at the Russia, Caucasus and Central Asia Centre at ISPI. Prior to that, she was a Marie Curie Fellow based at the Middle East Technical University in Ankara, Turkey, where she has also pursued her PhD. She was a Visiting Fellow at the Saint

Petersburg State University and at the London headquarters of the ECFR. She has also worked as a junior researcher at the Brussels office of FRIDE and as a research assistant at CIDOB in Barcelona.

Eliza Tanner Hawkins received her PhD in Journalism and Mass Communication from the University of Wisconsin-Madison. She currently studies issues surrounding democracy and media.

Ilke Toygür is an Analyst of European Affairs at Elcano Royal Institute and an Adjunct Professor of Political Science at Carlos III University of Madrid. Her main research areas include European politics, elections in Europe, Turkish politics and Turkey-EU relations. She has been a Visiting Researcher at the European University Institute and University of Mannheim and she was granted the prestigious "Mercator-IPC Fellowship" in Istanbul Policy Center.

www.ingramcontent.com/pod-product-compliance
Lightning Source LLC
Chambersburg PA
CBHW070806280326
41934CB00012B/3084